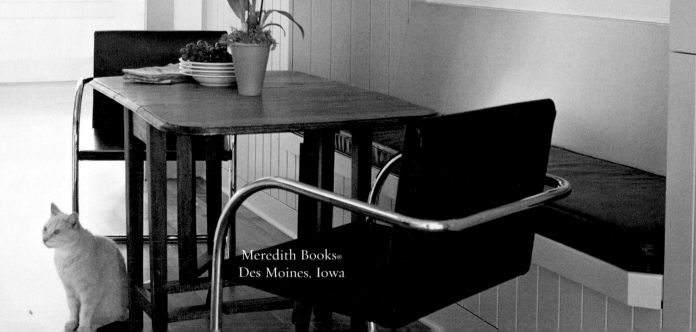

Better Homes and Gard

ADDING
CHARACTER
WITH ARCHITECTURAL DETAILS

Meredith Books®
Des Moines, Iowa

Better Homes and Gardens®
ADDING CHARACTER

Editor: Paula Marshall
Writer: Andria Hayday
Contributing Editors: Bernadette Baczynski, Cathy Long, Catherine Staub
Graphic Designers: Chris Conyers, Beth Runcie, Joe Wysong
  (Conyers Design, Inc.)
Copy Chief: Terri Fredrickson
Publishing Operations Manager: Karen Schirm
Edit and Design Production Coordinator: Mary Lee Gavin
Editorial Assistants: Kaye Chabot, Kairee Mullen
Marketing Product Managers: Aparna Pande, Isaac Petersen, Gina Rickert,
  Stephen Rogers, Brent Wiersma, Tyler Woods
Book Production Managers: Pam Kvitne, Marjorie J. Schenkelberg,
  Rick von Holdt, Mark Weaver
Contributing Copy Editor: Ira Lacher
Contributing Proofreaders: David Craft, Dan Degan, Sue Fetters
Cover Photographer: Colleen Duffley
Contributing Photographers: Susan Gilmore
Indexer: Kathleen Poole

MEREDITH® BOOKS
Executive Director, Editorial: Gregory H. Kayko
Executive Director, Design: Matt Strelecki
Executive Editor/Group Manager: Denise Caringer
Senior Associate Design Director: Mick Schnepf

Publisher and Editor in Chief: James D. Blume
Editorial Director: Linda Raglan Cunningham
Executive Director, Marketing: Jeffrey B. Myers
Executive Director, New Business Development: Todd M. Davis
Executive Director, Sales: Ken Zagor
Director, Operations: George A. Susral
Director, Production: Douglas M. Johnston
Business Director: Jim Leonard

Vice President and General Manager: Douglas J. Guendel

***BETTER HOMES AND GARDENS®* MAGAZINE**
Editor in Chief: Karol DeWulf Nickell
Deputy Editor, Home Design: Oma Blaise Ford

MEREDITH PUBLISHING GROUP
President: Jack Griffin
Senior Vice President: Bob Mate

MEREDITH CORPORATION
Chairman and Chief Executive Officer: William T. Kerr
President and Chief Operating Officer: Stephen M. Lacy

In Memoriam E.T. Meredith III (1933-2003)

Photo Credit: Column profile images on page 53, courtesy of Chadsworth's
1.800.Columns, 277 North Front St., Historic Wilmington, NC 28401;
www.columns.com

{CONTENTS}

ELEMENTS OF CHARACTER

Mass production is an efficient way to make widgets, but an inferior way to create homes. Yet Americans have filled town after town with "cookie-cutter" houses. Some are plain little boxes, others looming McMansions, or Townhomes from the Land of Taupe. But whatever the size, shape, or color, something is missing.

That something is character. A house with character is unique, reflecting its surroundings, its history, and the personality of those who call it home. Though we tend to associate character with older homes, this quality can be incorporated to a house of any age.

{DEFINING CHARACTER}

So what gives a house character? Character always results from careful attention to detail. Beauty is critical, but it takes more than mere decoration to create character.

Elements that add character imbue a home with a sense of permanence, quality, and comfort. These are *thoughtful* and *useful* details, where, as Frank Lloyd Wright put it, form and function unite. It's the built-in that solves storage problems with panache ... the window seat that creates an irresistible retreat ... trimwork that artfully changes our perception of a room's shape or substance ... a small window that captures a surprising view.

Just a few simple lines frame the windows and front door, but the effect is welcoming, and it quietly defines the home's style.

This book showcases an array of rooms, spaces, and houses with a rich sense of character. We'll help you identify what's missing from your home and offer inspired choices for completing the picture. Maybe you own an older home that has been stripped of its character. Or a newer one that never had it to begin with. Either way, you'll discover solutions both simple and grand, allowing you to develop a makeover strategy that's tailored to your house, your lifestyle, and your budget. And if you're building anew, you'll learn how to incorporate character from the start, creating a house that feels like home the moment you step inside the door.

DEVISING A PLAN Whatever the size of your house or your aspirations, three guidelines can help you build character successfully: Consider the big picture, work with the style you have, and be consistent.

Consider the big picture. Even if you intend to start with a few cosmetic changes to just one room, the best way to begin a makeover is to assess the overall picture. Planning with the long view in mind helps you set priorities and avoid a scattershot approach. Don't lose sight of the ultimate goal: a house with true character doesn't simply look better, it's also more comfortable and pleasing to live in.

Think about your home's strengths and weaknesses. Does your house take advantage of its best views and harmonize with its setting—with easy indoor-outdoor transitions—or does it feel disconnected from the world around it?

Look from room to room. Are they too cold or dark? Is the floor plan too choppy? Is there a pleasing balance between private and open spaces, cozy and expansive? What effect

Character isn't restricted to older houses or traditional settings. Built-ins, niches, and beautiful Douglas-fir trim suffuse this contemporary home with standout personality.

True to its Tudor roots, this foyer includes Gothic archways that rise to a central point instead of a smooth curve. The plank door with an arched top is another Tudor tradition.

Creative thinking turned an ordinary split-level into this classically detailed home. The new style gracefully folds into the house rather than fighting with the basic structure.

would a broader passage have? A French door ? A bigger window or a higher ceiling? The upcoming chapters are filled with solutions, but to choose the best one, you have to identify the problems first.

Work with what you have. Let your home's prevailing architectural style guide you in the choices you make. In short, don't try to make your home into something it's not. Instead consider changes that enhance and strengthen its style.

For example, if you're adding a porch to a home with Victorian flavor, turned spindles are compatible. On a Craftsman bungalow, flared piers and stout, square balusters are a better fit. If your home already has Tudor styling, play it up with classic Tudor touches, such as an arched, batten-style front door (with vertical planks), or heavy, rustic porch brackets. Inside you might transform a broad, squared-off passage into an archway. Be sensitive to the finer points of style.

Maybe you're lamenting, "But my house *has no style.*" That's probably an overstatement. Ranch houses and split-level homes are often maligned unfairly, but when it comes to makeovers, they do tend to be chameleons. Often they can assume many different styles successfully. Try to honor the spirit of the original house. A low-slung ranch with deep, sheltering eaves could wear Craftsman styling quite comfortably (see the Case Study on page 168) or take on a modern edge. And a squatter ranch with a more traditional shape (a steeper roof, a front-facing gable) could readily accept a classic cottage look.

Be consistent. From the type of millwork and door hardware to the style of built-ins to the prevailing type of

A blend of Prairie and Craftsman style, this home's flared piers and square columns repeat details from the front porch. Consistency of design both inside and out makes a house a more harmonious whole.

Symmetrical built-ins and clean lines give this Craftsman-inspired room a pleasing sense of order.

Properly scaled, an arched
window is a graceful addition
to a traditionally styled room.

11

When this loft was a warehouse, the large window was appropriate, but when the space became a home, the window was overwhelming. By dividing the window into three sections and flanking the whole unit with columns, the window grouping has a scale more in keeping with the room's function as living space.

ELEMENTS THAT ADD CHARACTER
INSTILL A SENSE OF PERMANENCE,
QUALITY, AND COMFORT.

window, every detail matters. And those details should match or complement one another throughout the home.

It would be wrong to say that mixing styles is always taboo. A cultural "melting pot," America encompasses a rich heritage of eclectic architecture, with homes that marry several compatible styles under one roof. But the key word is "compatible." Breaking design rules is a tricky business.

UNDERSTANDING DESIGN Much like a painting, each wall (or facade) of your home is a composition in which every element—a window, a door, an area set off by a trim line—is a basic shape, and the outer boundaries are the frame. Whether a composition is two-dimensional or three-dimensional, it involves the same basic principles of design. And its ability to please the eye or prompt a grimace depends on how well those principles are used.

Scale. Scale is a relative concept. A pair of columns that looks grand on a neoclassic house might seem ostentatious and overbearing when squeezed onto the stoop of a low-slung ranch. Likewise, a deep, built-up cornice might be perfectly proportioned in a room with 9-foot ceilings. But if the ceiling drops even a foot, the same trim looks too heavy.

Your own size affects your sense of scale as well. If you're relatively short, you may be quite comfortable standing below a 7-foot-high soffit. But if you're 6-feet 6-inches, the experience is completely different.

13

Line. In basic geometry, lines are always straight, but when designers speak of line, they also include connections that are flowing, such as a sinewy curve or a graceful arch.

Lines are interesting because of what they accomplish. Strong vertical lines emphasize height, while horizontal lines can make an object or a room seem broader than it is. Curves are soft, recalling organic forms, and offering visual relief from rigid angles. Diagonal lines are dynamic, often conveying a sense of motion.

Balance. There are two basic types of balance: symmetrical (or formal) and asymmetrical (or informal). In a *symmetrical* arrangement, all of the elements to the right of an invisible center "line" mirror those on the left. It's a very classic and traditional look, illustrated by matching columns that flank a door, or identical urns that flank a walk. Used effectively, symmetry creates a very strong, stable impression.

In an *asymmetrical* composition, the objects on either side of the center line are different, but when you view each side as a group, they still balance one another. For instance, two smaller objects on the left can balance a larger element on the right— the way a pair of dormers might balance an off-center entry gable. And a small, dark object placed on a mantel can balance a larger, paler object on the opposite side. Asymmetrical arrangements tend to be more casual than their symmetrical counterparts. Because they offer more surprises, however, they can be visually exciting.

Visual weight. In design, appearances are everything. Bigger objects look weightier and a column appears lighter on top if it's tapered. Color—and to a lesser extent, texture—affect optical weight as well, since dark shades are heavier than pale tints. That's why when you paint a ceiling dark or cover it

with rustic wood planks, it suddenly seems lower. Positioning is also a factor: An object that's set back from others is less prominent, and therefore visually lighter. For example, a two-story addition that lines up with the front of a house can loom like a bully, but if you push it back from the facade, it seems less imposing.

Rhythm. Designers often compare architecture to music. Just as a musical composition has a rhythm—a pattern created by the repetition of notes—architecture and interior design create a visual rhythm.

Think about the way single windows "march" across the front of a Georgian house. The balustrade on a traditional porch rail can resemble a series of staccato notes, and by introducing a larger element—Tuscan columns, for instance— you can change the rhythm. Spacing affects rhythm as well, serving as a visual pause between objects.

Repetition and Variation. When elements—especially shapes, materials, and colors—are repeated in a design, they become stronger. Repetition lends unity and harmony to a composition. Like musical variations on a theme, fresh twists to a familiar pattern keep visual compositions from becoming boring. A strong theme or a defining motif provides continuity, while variety adds a refreshing element of surprise.

Restraint. Admittedly, knowing when enough is enough can be a matter of taste. To those who admire the serenity of Asian design, for instance, Victorian spindlework might seem a bit overwrought, while to others it's the epitome of charm. But in good design the old adages still apply: Less is usually more, and quality is more important than quantity. Without restraint, nothing seems special.

This daringly cantilevered stairway climbs to the highest levels of craftsmanship. Shadows on the wall repeat the visual rhythm of its stunning balustrade.

A HOUSE WITH CHARACTER IS UNIQUE, REFLECTING ITS SURROUNDINGS, ITS HISTORY, AND THE PERSONALITY OF THOSE WHO CALL IT HOME.

The bank of same-size windows adds a strong horizontal element that helps to visually anchor a high-ceilinged room. Clever use of standard windows like this creates a custom look.

{ DREAMS vs. DOLLARS }

Dream homes are lovely to behold, but for many of us, reality is a tight budget. Fortunately, not every fix has to be expensive. One of the simplest ways to add character to your home is upgrading millwork: adding or changing molding treatments, or replacing the doors and hardware. Millwork can add drama to a ceiling as well, which is a far less expensive change than altering its structure. One well-chosen window (a single porthole in a foyer, a small art-glass window on a stair landing) can make a small space more special. An outdoor room is much less costly than a four-season addition, but it can be even more enjoyable—while vastly improving the character of the rooms that adjoin it.

Those are just a sampling of ideas you'll find in the pages to come. The point is this: If you shop carefully, seek out creative solutions, and follow the principles of good design, character needn't come with a huge price tag.

This kitchen gets an old-world look on a budget. The "planked" walls are really fiberboard that's been routed and painted. Open shelves with sturdy brackets add style and storage, but cost much less than cabinets. Even the limestone flooring has a budget-wise edge: The 12-inch-square tiles were set by the homeowners.

MOLDING, COLUMNS, WAINSCOTING, ETC.

Beautiful moldings, charming wainscoting, graceful columns—elements like these help make a house a more inviting and satisfying refuge. Many details are cosmetic rather than structural, yet when they're thoughtfully designed, they become part of the very fiber of the house, enhancing its architectural identity. Luckily, such fine details are relatively simple to add, and with high-quality craftsmanship and materials, they can give any home greater presence, grace, and style.

{INTERIOR TRIM}

Like many architectural traditions, trim can be traced to ancient Greece. Imagine the ruins of a Greek temple with a dentil pattern stretching over the top of an elaborate frieze, or egg-and-dart molding beneath a cornice. Such classic designs, painstakingly hand-carved in stone, inspired the elaborate plasterwork and hardwood moldings that followed.

By the Victorian Era, wood moldings had become so popular that homeowners pored through pattern books, combining piece after piece in impressive built-up designs. The Arts and Crafts Era ushered in a less fussy approach to woodwork, but only in the sleek homes of the International Modernist Movement was the notion that a house needed interior trim to look finished cast aside altogether.

In the postwar building boom, as ranch-style and split-level homes sprouted up, moldings became less substantial and cornices disappeared altogether. Today many homeowners are correcting the problem by changing or embellishing the trim. Few home improvements can do so much to transform the character of a room with so little commitment of time, energy, or expense.

Left: Classically inspired moldings are an integral part of this Georgian home's identity. Note the dentil pattern that adorns the cornice and reappears beneath the mantel shelf.

Above right: Lighter and less expensive than finely carved wood, polyurethane molding makes sense for an elaborate crown. In a lofty position, it won't be closely scrutinized and is subjected to very few bumps or scrapes.

Right: Broad, flat trim is the handsome hallmark of an Arts and Crafts interior.

Above: Art Deco currents flow through this Craftsman home, whose cornice treatment includes "stepped out" layers of flat trim. Vertical accents provide visual rhythm.

Right: It looks upscale, but every element in this classic trim suite can be ordered through your local lumber or home improvement store. Note how all the elements work together: Without the paneled wainscoting, the wall treatment would be overbearing. The entablature atop the door gives the door height and weight to keep it in scale and keeping with the entire look.

Placed at the corners of door and window casings, a rosette is a traditional Victorian element that adds panache while simplifying joinery.

WHAT TRIM DOES Trim has a practical side: It conceals less-than-perfect joints between walls and floors or ceilings, and covers gaps between door or window jambs and surrounding surfaces. It also protects the softer wall surface (plaster or drywall) from bumps, bangs, and nailings. For instance, a chair rail forms a defensive line against chairbacks that are pushed against a wall.

To most of us, however, trim is important because of the way it affects the look of a room, adding warmth and visual interest. By underscoring the fundamental construction, it also has a way of seeming structural even when it's not.

One of the most impressive tricks of trim is its ability to change our perceptions of a room's size and shape. By creating a strong line that draws our eye around a room, it can often make a room feel larger. Conversely, by breaking up a soaring wall into multiple sections or adding visual weight to a ceiling, it can make a room feel cozier. It's all a matter of line, weight, and proportion.

Modular bookcases become stately built-ins when they're trimmed out like this. A round window offers a pleasant visual surprise.

23

{ TYPES OF TRIM }

Trimwork is made up of many separate pieces, so it helps to learn the options. On these two pages you'll find many of the possible elements in a suite of trim (a room's entire package of trimwork). A room need not include every element, of course—in most cases, that's not even desirable. Baseboards often go "shoeless," for example, especially when the room is carpeted. Door casings can stretch to the floor without a plinth block. And while a traditional house with high ceilings might wear both a chair rail and a picture rail, in a more modestly scaled space, limiting the suite to just one of these horizontal bands usually creates a better look.

CASING. Trim that frames a door or window, fitting flat against the wall.

PLINTH BLOCK. The block on which a pilaster rests. It simulates the column's base.

BASEBOARD, SHOE, AND BASE CAP. A baseboard covers the joint between the floor and wall, hiding any gaps at the edge of tile work, carpet, or floorboards. The shoe—a separate, much smaller piece—is typically quarter round. A common three-part baseboard treatment includes a shoe, a broad piece of base molding with a flat upper edge, plus a narrow base cap.

CORNER BLOCK (ROSETTE). A decorative square piece that may appear at the upper corners of doors and windows, with casing butted against it. Corner blocks eliminate the need for complicated corner joints.

PILASTER. A decorative half-column set directly against a wall—or trim that's designed to mimic a column. The door casing in neoclassic treatments is often a pilaster.

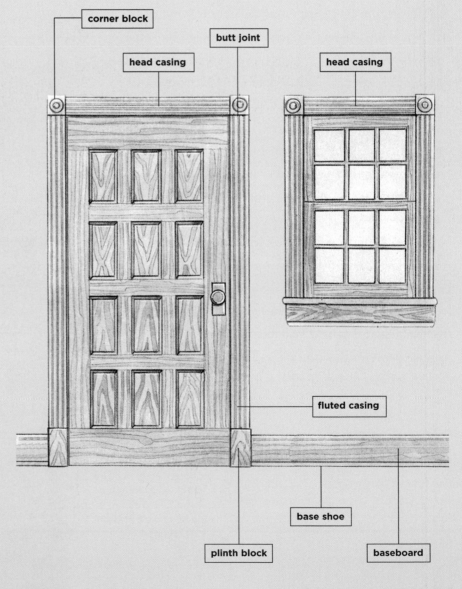

corner block

head casing

butt joint

head casing

fluted casing

base shoe

plinth block

baseboard

{PROFILES}

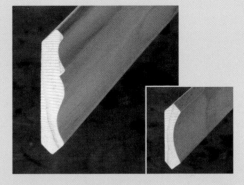

Chair rail. Typically 30 to 36 inches from the floor (a third of the wall's height), this horizontal band of trim can appear alone or atop wainscoting. It draws the eye around a room—an effect that can make a small room seem larger.

Ranch. The straightforward line and taper of ranch molding reflect the clean lines associated with—and therefore are well suited to—modern ranch-style homes. Also called clamshell molding.

Cornice (crown). Trim spanning the joint between the wall and ceiling. The terms "crown" and "cornice" are often used interchangeably, but crown molding is also a specific group of vaguely S-shape profiles that rest at an angle, slanting toward the room's interior. Available in both narrow and wide depths, crown molding often tops window and door treatments and appears on fireplace mantels, repeating the style of the ceiling cornice. Sometimes a cornice is made from cove molding, which has a C-shape contour.

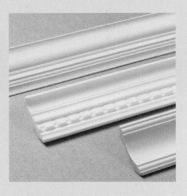

Wainscoting cap or ply cap. This piece of molding serves as a finishing piece for wainscoting. It conceals the top edge of the panels.

Half round. This utilitarian style of molding is often used as a finishing detail or as part of a more elaborate build, for example, under a chair rail or along the front edge of a shelf.

Quarter round. Another utilitarian molding, quarter round serves a similar role to half round. It can be used at the ceiling or wall to add a shadow line to a crown molding, or to conceal an inside seam on a wall.

Plastic, foam, and vinyl. An easy way to get a detailed or complicated molding is to buy precast moldings made of lightweight materials.

A nod to Asian simplicity, a broad band of flat oak trim is a unifying element in this remodeled ranch home. Paired vertical bands highlight focal points such as a fireplace, as shown here, or window groupings.

MATERIALS AND FINISHES When choosing new trim, think about the finish first. Will it be painted, stained, or left natural? The answer helps shape your choice of materials. Wood is the traditional choice, and its beauty and charm are undeniable.

Wood isn't your only option, however. If you're painting trim, manufactured materials such as medium-density fiberboard (MDF) can be highly convincing stand-ins for wood. Polyurethane moldings have the advantage of being lightweight (making them popular choices for ornate cornices), and they don't shrink the way wood does. They're often bendable as well.

If you plan to stain wood trim or simply seal it to preserve its natural beauty, the type of wood you choose becomes vitally important. Grain is not the only consideration; each variety of wood also has an inherent color, which makes an impact on your decor. (For more details on woods and their characteristics, see pages 180-181)

While you're shopping, you'll invariably come across "paint-grade" wood trim, which is less expensive than higher grades. A length of paint-grade molding is formed from smaller pieces of wood, united by finger joints. They're strong, but the overall effect is a bit patchy. That's why it's best to finish such molding with paint.

Top above: Wood rounds give simple sconces an elegant foundation.

Above: Topped by a slender cap, the wall paneling continues onto adjoining walls, where it becomes high wainscoting.

Left: An upgrade to bare walls and a lonely fireplace, this well-tailored living room features paneling made of paint-grade plywood trimmed with 1×6 boards and quarter round molding.

Trim is the glue that holds an open plan together. The moldings in this kitchen and family room are virtually identical, apart from their contrasting finishes.

{ CONSISTENCY IS THE SUREST WAY TO ACHIEVE VISUAL HARMONY. }

DESIGN FUNDAMENTALS Consistency is the surest way to achieve visual harmony and give your home a sense of architectural integrity. The closer the link between rooms, the more important a uniform treatment becomes.

Consistency doesn't have to be a straitjacket, however. It's very common to start with a basic, defining scheme for trim—one that will extend throughout adjoining rooms—and then add to it in formal areas. For instance, you may extend a chair rail across your family room and continue it into the dining room where paneled wainscoting appears below it. In the living room, perhaps you'll panel the entire wall, echoing the chair rail by continuing the same line as a reference.

Here are a few additional tips for designing with trim:

Balance the cornice and base. If one is a bit heavier, it's typically the baseboard, which plays the role of a visual pedestal or foundation for the wall. An oversize cornice can make a wall look top heavy, threatening to topple it.

Consider ceiling heights. The lower the ceiling, the subtler the molding treatment. As a general rule for crown molding, choose a maximum depth of three-quarter inch for every vertical foot of wall. That means a standard 8-foot ceiling should wear a cornice no more than 6 inches deep. Deeper crowns can be overwhelming and make the ceiling appear lower. (Conversely, a 6-inch molding can feel lost on a 10-foot ceiling.)

Avoid busy treatments in small spaces. You'll only make the space seem smaller. However, a full suite of trim can look elegant in a small space if you de-emphasize the patterns. Paint trim and paneling the same shade as the wall. That creates a subtler, more textural effect.

Experiment with samples. Buy sample pieces of trim and experiment with built-up combinations. To check proportions, there's no substitute for field testing. Apply samples to the wall to see how these combinations actually look in your rooms.

Remember the joints. The depth of trim—the thickness of its cross section—is important, especially where different elements come together. A plinth should extend farther from the wall than the door casing it supports. Door casings are usually thicker than baseboards. Similarly, a chair rail must extend far enough from the wall to cap off any board, batten, or paneling that rises to meet it.

Right: White paint lightens and brightens the fairly elaborate door trim and cornice piece.

Far right: Decorative carved blocks add visual interest and break up the long lines of this door molding.

A pretty rope detail makes this built-up cornice a cut above the ordinary.

"RESHAPING" A ROOM Trim can change your perception of a room's shape. For instance, to make a high-ceilinged room feel cozier, install a picture rail several inches below the cornice. Paint the area between them a contrasting color to add weight to the frieze, drawing it downward. Some additional ideas:

Stretch door trim from the top of the door to the ceiling, creating a simple entablature treatment, to make a room's ceiling seem taller.

Wipe a subtly darker shade of finish in the crevices of fluted or reeded trim to draw attention to the lines.

Add panel molding to the ceiling of an overly long room. Install the trim to outline a faux soffit, placing it farther from the ceiling's edge at the ends of the room. The room will feel shorter.

Extend a door. A standard-height door (6 foot, 8 inches) can look too short in a tall room. To balance proportions, install a beefier entablature above the door. Use a complementary treatment for windows.

Cozy up a vaulted ceiling. Install crown molding or a picture rail a little below the natural ceiling line. Or panel the entire ceiling with warm wood; the ceiling will feel lower.

Opposite: Skimping on trim was unthinkable when this Victorian rowhouse was constructed. Note the fluted trim and rosettes.

Right: Dark wood planks visually lower a lofty ceiling, bringing warmth and a more human scale to the room.

{ MATTERS OF STYLE }

As architectural styles have evolved through the years, so too have the corresponding styles of interior trim. Here's a quick tour of popular categories:

Classic and neoclassic. Designs from this group celebrate the graceful forms and careful proportions of Greek and Roman architecture. For example, casings flanking a doorway form pilasters, echoing the base and capital of a classical column. Doors and windows may be topped with entablatures, and picture rails define a frieze. Trim is typically painted to emulate the paleness of marble.

Colonial. Rooted in post-and-beam construction, colonial designs embrace a number of historic regional styles, both rustic and formal. Beamed ceilings and raised-panel wainscoting were popular, and while trim was sometimes stained, it was often painted in a palette that included dusky grayish blues and deep brownish reds.

Victorian. Highbrow Victorians gravitated toward richly stained hardwoods. With tall rooms as their canvas, they indulged a passion for ornamentation, creating everything from foot-deep crowns to fully paneled walls to frilly fretwork atop open doorways. Corner rosette blocks were extremely popular.

Arts and Crafts. The Arts and Crafts Movement began in England and continued in the United States, where it became entwined with Craftsman and Prairie architecture. Although there were differences, the fundamental tenets called for a return to clean lines, spare geometry, and "honest" natural materials.

Above top: Corinthian columns and an elaborately decorated frieze represent the frillier side of neoclassic design.

Above: The earthy wood tone and straightforward geometry in this dining room clearly reflect the no-nonsense aesthetic of the Arts and Crafts Movement.

ATTENTION TO DETAIL In trimwork, fine details matter. Often it's the subtle differences between two treatments that determine their relative beauty—the amount of overhang that a header casing might be given in an Arts and Crafts treatment, for instance. The amount of reveal (see page 37) adds yet another fine detail—and another shadow line—that contributes to the overall look of the room.

Built-up trim doesn't have to be ornate or overly thick. If you use slender pieces, the result won't be overbearing, even in a small room. In fact just adding a simple 1-inch backband around clamshell molding can make a tremendous difference in its appearance.

Planks connect the cornice with the door trim in this Arts and Crafts home. Even when painted, the wide-plank trim clearly denotes the style.

When it wears the right "hat," a deep chair rail can double as a picture ledge, offering casual gallery space while visually expanding a room.

{JOINERY 101}

Every trim project involves fitting pieces of wood together. How complex the joint depends on placement and finish. For example, exposed wood crown molding often requires precise coping and miter cuts at the corners because any gaps will be very noticeable. If the molding were to be painted, a mitered joint that can be perfected with filler could be a suitable—and less time-consuming—choice. Here's a short overview of basic joinery:

Butt joint: When a piece of trim is chopped off squarely at the end and pushed or "butted" against another, it forms a butt joint. Butt joints are among the simplest woodworking joints to make, provided the underlying surfaces are square and true.

Scarf joint: When a trim line stretches across a wall's entire face (a chair rail, for instance), trim often has to be pieced together end to end. Each end is cut with a complementary angle so the pieces can overlap. That way, if the trim expands or contracts, you won't have an unsightly gap.

Miter joint: Look at an upper corner on a window or door casing, and you're likely to see a miter joint. The top and side pieces of trim are cut at a 45-degree angle, and then fit together like a picture frame.

Coping joint: A coping joint allows a line of contoured trim that wraps a room (crown molding, for instance) to merge gracefully in an inside corner. The first piece is cut square and simply butted against the intersecting wall. The end of the second piece is carefully shaped with a saw and a file—"coped"—to match the trim's outward contours.

FINESSE POINTS: THE TWO R'S.

Returns and reveals represent two finesse techniques that can make or break a project.

Reveal: Before a door or window is trimmed out, you can see the wood jambs that box the opening. When finish carpenters frame the opening with casing, they leave a little bit of each jamb exposed. That exposed portion is called a reveal. Usually just an eighth-inch to a quarter-inch wide, the reveal creates a subtle shadow line with a significant impact.

Return: Created from a very small, mitered piece of trim, it allows the contoured profile to continue around the corner of the molding and "return" back to the wall.

When your trim style is relatively simple, a finely sanded edge or a beveled cut on the end may be all you need to create a graceful transition to the wall. But for a truly ornate, elegant treatment with a finished look, returns are mandatory. One of the most obvious uses of a return is the corner of a fireplace mantel.

{WAINSCOTING, PLANKS, & PANELS}

Tongue and groove. Board and batten. Raised panel. Beaded board. Picture frame. This is the language of a well-dressed wall—and just a sampling of the many options for covering a wall with millwork. Depending on the style of the house, the effect may be casual or formal, rustic or refined, traditional or contemporary. But in every case, millwork surface treatments can add charm and texture to a room.

Left: Designs for picture frames (or "wall frames") can be minimal, like this low wainscoting, or they can cover a wall completely, framing art and highlighting architectural features. Frame sizes often vary as they march around a room, but the spacing between them should generally be uniform. For a subtler, more textural effect, paint moldings to match the wall.

Right: Flat-panel wainscoting is a traditional Arts and Crafts treatment. For details on creating this look, see page 183.

Rough-hewn planks at two-thirds wall height lend textural beauty to this old-fashioned bath. The shallow display shelf offers ample storage space and creates a roost for flickering votives.

Topped by a display shelf and a peg rail, this 5½-foot-high wainscoting is as practical as it is pretty. The oak 1×6 planks are whitewashed with water-thinned latex paint to let the grain show through. Chamfered edges on each plank accentuate vertical lines.

The most popular wall treatment is *wainscoting,* which covers only part of the wall. Low wainscoting rises to meet the chair rail, forming an element that classicists call a *dado.* High wainscoting roughly covers two-thirds of the wall's height. Popular in both colonial and Arts and Crafts styles, it's often capped by a *plate rail,* where plates can be displayed on edge. (If you display china at chair-rail height, you'll soon be sweeping up the pieces.) A groove in the top of the rail secures the plates.

PICTURE FRAMES are a treatment that mimics the look of wall panels. (See page 38 for an example.) Narrow strips of molding are applied directly to the wall, either as wainscoting or full-height paneling. The shapes and sizes of the frames may be fairly uniform, or they may vary to create a more pleasing pattern or to emphasize other architectural features. The spacing between them is usually fixed, and upper edges of adjacent frames are carefully aligned. Picture frames are less expensive than traditional wall panels, but they're not a lesser-grade imitation—many elegant historic homes received exactly this treatment.

The surrounding pages offer a gallery of ideas for adding panels, planked walls, and wainscoting to your decor. For do-it-yourselfers, we've gathered instructions for the simpler projects and included them at the back of this book.

Beaded-board wainscoting exudes classic cottage style.
Although tongue-and-groove boards are the traditional
ingredient, ready-made panels mimic the look for less, and
they're much easier to install. (See page 186 for instructions.)

Above: Applied horizontally, simple beaded board is an effective surface treatment for an old-fashioned bedroom beneath the eaves.

Left: Reminiscent of a classic wooden fence, lattice wainscoting brings garden flavor to a foyer. For a polished installation, remember this rule: Top and bottom rails must be thick enough to fit flush with or protrude beyond the latticework between them.

43

{A WELL-DRESSED CEILING}

Beams, panels, and planks add texture and interest to a plain, flat ceiling and lend much-needed warmth to a soaring vault. Many of the treatments you'd apply to a wall work equally well overhead. That's why some designers call the ceiling your "fifth wall." Here are a few ideas for dressing it up:

Picture molding applied to the ceiling adds a distinctive layer of detail to this classically appointed room.

Create faux panels by installing an extra layer of drywall and cutting out rectangles to create recessed areas. Trim the cut edges of the drywall with narrow molding.

Mimic the look of a coffered ceiling with flat trim and molding. Paint the trim and ceiling panels the same color for a more elegant textural effect, or hang hollow boxed beams from the joists. Made from 2×4s wrapped with handsome hardwood 1-bys, boxed beams offer the look of real beams without the weight and expense.

Hang recycled barn beams for an Early American flavor. They're heavy, so consult a qualified professional who can judge whether the floor joists overhead can handle the extra load.

Install tongue-and-groove wood planking for warmth. In a cottage-style house, painted beaded board is a fresh alternative.

A perfect finish to a beautiful room, this coffered ceiling features boxed beams edged with deep crown molding.

45

A word of caution: Don't get carried away with decorating. If a ceiling treatment is dark or busy, it can make an already low ceiling seem even lower. Furthermore, if every ceiling in your house looks different, your home won't have a sense of integrity or quality, no matter how much you spend. Reserve special treatments for important spaces—a foyer, for instance, or adjoining living areas—and make sure they complement the other ceilings in your home. Competing treatments seriously diminish the overall effect.

Left: "X" marks the ceiling! Beaded-board insets and planks edged with narrow molding transform a formerly ho-hum bedroom. A stylish fan boosts the style quotient and accents the center point.

Below left: Warm wood planks enrich this bedroom's vaulted ceiling. To maintain the cozy scale, a matching line of crown molding continues beneath the peaked gable.

Below: Painted "Charleston blue" to recall the sky, a high, paneled ceiling comes into focus and adds visual punch to a white kitchen. Same-color panels and trim emphasize texture and pattern.

These decorative beams received an instant aging technique when they were added to a new East Coast home. You can readily replicate the effect: Start with newly rough-sawn beams (green wood cracks as it dries). Stain a dark brown, then apply whitewash for a mottled look.

47

{DOORS}

Set at opposite sides of an entry hall, arch-top doors offer an elegant introduction to this updated Mediterranean-style house. Simple flat panels, clean lines, and sleek hardware signal the homeowners' contemporary tastes.

Double pocket doors add drama to a broad passage. A sunny yellow paint scheme staves off winter blues in this house filled with old-fashioned Swedish flavor. Note the two-tone paneled door across the hall.

A pocket door with frosted glass panels lets a bath and bedroom share light while preserving both privacy and floor space.

The need for doors is an open-and-shut case. Portals that link one space to another, they create vital connections when open, admitting light, views, and breezes, as well as people and pets. When closed, solid doors create privacy, while glass-panel doors continue to share views and light.

Although the functional role of doors is pretty obvious, doors are also important for aesthetic reasons. Like windows, they're a key part of any wall's composition, and they're often focal points. That's why architectural designers choose a door style with great care and continue it throughout the house. Slab doors suit contemporary homes, but so do doors with large, flat panels and minimal molding. Raised panels

WITH HIGH-QUALITY CRAFTSMANSHIP AND MATERIALS, ARCHITECTURAL DETAILS CAN GIVE ANY HOME GREATER PRESENCE, GRACE, AND STYLE.

Left: French doors aren't the only light-sharing solution for interior spaces. Here, a sliding door with frosted glass pairs with matching fixed panels in a contemporary home with Asian currents. Shutters atop a plate glass window echo the door's styling.

Above: A salvaged door suspended from a barn-style track creates a sliding entry to a walk-in closet. Like the painted door to the right, its four-panel styling suits the traditional flavor of the house. Note the black hardware and hinges.

look traditional, but the choices go well beyond the popular six-panel colonial style, and each variation has a unique flavor. A two-panel door can be an elegant choice, for instance, and when the panels are vertical, the door seems taller. Board-and-batten-style doors have a rustic old-world flavor, but with the proper hardware, doors with sleekly painted vertical planks can feel equally at home in a contemporary setting.

All this attention to detail doesn't mean every door has to be fancy. In fact, excessive ornamentation on doors detracts from other elements in the home, and can make a house feel "tarted up." It's often the substance of the door, defined by the quality of its construction and materials, that matters most. Light and flimsy, hollow-core doors simply don't have the character of solid wood.

Rustic plank doors with simple bracing at the top and bottom contribute to the character of this Mediterranean-style home. (In an early colonial decor, a Z-brace is a common embellishment.)

{HARDWARE: JEWELRY FOR DOORS}

Basic brass doorknobs look good in most settings, but distinctive hardware can truly set your home apart. Consider alternate materials and shapes. Lever-style handles are easier to open than knobs and look stylish as well. Black knobs suit an Early American decor, and hammered bronze complements Craftsman-style homes. Victorian knobs were often just as ornate as the rest of the house, with beautiful long escutcheons (back plates that fit flat against the door). Experiment: Try different hardware and see which suits your doors best. Some websites even let you choose a door style and swap hardware on the computer screen as easily as you might change earrings or cufflinks.

Don't forget the hinges: You'll view them every time the door is left open, and even notice them when it's shut. A rustic colonial door would not be the same without its black strap hinges. Traditional knob-and-pin hinges subtly distinguish older interior doors, and they can be the right touches when you're starting a door makeover.

Though the same basic style of hardware usually extends throughout a house, it's appropriate to embellish a special door. A front entry, the door to a master bath, a passage to a personal retreat—all of these can benefit from distinctive treatments.

{COLUMNS}

When we speak of post-and-beam architecture, we usually think of rustic barns and beautifully crafted homes with open interiors and stunning natural woodwork. But the temples of ancient Greece were essentially post and beam too: The "posts" were simply columns made of stone.

In modern architecture, columns are often decorative rather than structural, but to the eye, that rarely matters. The sculptural beauty of columns is what we value most, and the mere impression of strength is pleasing. The Greeks demanded that there always be an even number of columns at the front of a temple, and columns still tend to look best in twos. So do pilasters (decorative partial columns projecting from a wall).

When it comes to choosing a style of interior column, look to your home's exterior. If you spy one of the Classical Orders (see the sidebar),

Above right: Warmer than white, pine structural columns do the heavy lifting for a hallway's open "wall."

Right: A kitchen island forms the base of these Tuscan columns. Trimmed-out pedestals conceal hard working supports on either side of the bookshelves.

{ THE CLASSICAL ORDERS }

In their quest for ideal beauty, the Greeks created three basic styles, or Orders, for columns and the assemblies they supported: Doric, Ionic, and Corinthian. Ever the creative conquerors, the Romans adapted all three Orders, tweaking each design. (For instance, the Roman Doric column has a base and plinth; the Greek Doric column does not.) The Romans also invented two Orders all their own: Tuscan, which is very plain but elegant, and Composite, a marriage of Ionic and Corinthian styles.

Each Order is distinguished by the style of the top, or capital, of the column. The Greeks and Romans also adhered to very strict rules for proportions—all which contributed to the "rightness" and beauty of a building. Doric columns, the stoutest form, made long, horizontal buildings like the Parthenon look masculine and strong. Ionic and Corinthian columns are fluted and more slender, and they often adorned the temples of goddesses. Whatever the Order, each column is visibly wider at the base than at the top, with a graceful "swell" in between.

During the 1500s, an Italian stonemason named Andrea Palladio carefully studied the rules behind the Roman Orders and documented them. Modern architects still look to those rules for examples of pleasing scale and proportions.

Images courtesy of Chadsworth's 1.800.Columns

Doric

Ionic

Corinthian

Tuscan

Composite

A stout, square column, clean-lined pedestal, and a half-wall with a cabinet and leaded glass doors are a classic combination from the Arts and Crafts era.

for instance, consider repeating that style inside. It will give your home a greater sense of integrity and an identity that isn't abruptly divided at the threshold.

Not all columns fit the classical mold, however. Prairie-style columns are often stout and square, with flat-panel frames stretching along each side. Bungalow-style columns might be square with flared bases. A modern "column" might be a post wrapped in anigre wood boards with simple copper banding defining a capital. For a rustic cabin, you might substitute a stripped log or even a gnarly dead tree (without the eye-poking branches, of course).

Columns need not stretch from the floor to ceiling either. Where greater separation between spaces is desired, a half wall topped with a column is a fine solution.

ARCHITECTURAL CENTERPIECES

Among the many details that set the tone and style of a house, three stand apart: fireplaces, staircases, and built-ins. All have the potential to become architectural centerpieces. The fireplace, moreover, is a rallying point for family life, the staircase a sculptural nexus, the built-in adds function while maximizing the expression of a home's style. Granted a dramatic or special treatment, these elements don't merely anchor a room, they can anchor an entire home.

{FIREPLACES}

There's something mesmerizing about the dance of a flame, and when you add the crackle of burning wood, the glow of embers and an occasional spark, it's unmistakably romantic. It's no wonder many people view a fireplace as a necessity.

In an early colonial home, all activities centered on the hearth, where meals were prepared and winter clothing was hung to dry. But a fireplace offered more than just physical comfort. A place for gathering 'round, it provided spiritual comfort too.

Today's fireplaces have the same allure, and thanks to modern manufacturing methods, they are available in an ever-increasing array of designs and styles. Whether you're planning to add a new fireplace or remodeling an existing hearth, this chapter will help you find the solution that's right for your home.

Left: Handsome oak pillars frame a lavish wall of handcrafted tile in an Arts-and-Crafts-style inglenook. Literally a nook for a large open fire (*ingle* in Scots-Gaelic), it includes built-in benches on either side.

Above: A raised firebox ensures the flames are highly visible in this Swedish-style parlor. A hand-painted niche dips into the tiled surround and eliminates the need for additional artwork.

Nestled in a corner, an L-shape fireplace anchors a seating arrangement without blocking backyard views. The extended hearth doubles as seating and merges with surrounding shelves. Baskets for kindling and newspaper tuck below.

Above left: A see-through gas fireplace serves this master bedroom and an adjacent sitting area.

Above: An adobe or stucco exterior and a beehive shape distinguish the kiva-style fireplace. Most are positioned in a corner with banquettes on either side. Prefab kits are available.

TYPES OF FIREPLACES Largely the decorative choices——position, shape, and size; the style of its mantel, surround, and hearth—determine a fireplace's character. Here's a quick rundown of the options:

Placement. At one time, most fireplaces sat at the center of a humble one-room house. Today you can position a fireplace virtually anywhere. Kiva-style fireplaces—distinctive beehive-shape fireplaces of the American Southwest—are traditionally in a corner, but you can give nearly any style of fireplace the same angle. Squared away in a corner, a fireplace can be L-shape, with a firebox whose opening runs parallel to both walls. Although fireplaces are traditionally centered on an outside wall, placement on an interior wall offers many more options. Such a fireplace can share a chimney with one in the adjacent room, creating back-to-back hearths with separate fireboxes. Or the fireplace could be see-through, sharing its firebox and a view of its flames with two rooms.

Facings. Fireboxes may have rectangular openings, or they can be arched. The hearth can be flush with the floor, or raised, allowing the front hearth to double as seating. A raised hearth is often easier to view, making this a good choice if you'd like to enjoy the fire from an adjoining room. Raised hearths are also popular in formal dining rooms, where the table might otherwise block views, as well as master bedrooms and baths.

Space Dividers. Although most fireplaces are set within a wall, some of them become the wall, defining space in an otherwise open plan. The contemporary fireplace above is a prime example: a see-through gas unit, it's the only barrier between a master bedroom and the adjoining sitting room. Another option is to position the fireplace at the end of a peninsula. A three-sided fireplace offers more viewing points than a traditional hearth while gently dividing two spaces.

A wall of raised paneling surrounds this early colonial hearth, festooned for an old-fashioned holiday. Note the layered mantel shelf, which steps outward in stages. Angled walls in the firebox help project heat into the room.

ADDING A WOOD-BURNING FIREPLACE For enduring charm and classic beauty, a wood-burning fireplace crafted by a mason is unmatched. Traditional masonry can run upwards of $10,000, depending on the design and your geographic location (urban vs. rural). Stone and brick fireplaces also add staggering weight to a structure, which must be reinforced to carry the load. As convection carries smoke directly up the chimney, most of the fire's heat is carried right along with it. Moreover, as the fire dies down, heat from the surrounding room typically escapes up the chimney too.

You don't have to give up the sights and sounds of a traditional wood fire to gain a more efficient or less expensive fireplace, however. Today many remodelers choose a prefabricated or manufactured fireplace. Typically made of metal, these wood-burning units include both the firebox and flue, along with flashing and a chimney cap. The firebox is usually lined with ceramic panels that resemble firebrick. You add everything else—including the mantel and perhaps a veneered chimney in whatever style suits your fancy.

Prefab fireplaces have a number of advantages over traditional units. A zero-clearance fireplace has an insulated firebox and flue that can safely cozy up to combustible materials such as wood framing, often with just 1 or 2 inches of clearance. For efficiency, air for combustion is often drawn into the firebox from the outside, where a sophisticated chamber design burns fuel more completely than a traditional fireplace. Air from inside the room may circulate around the closed firebox to better heat the room. And newer models have a clean facade (eliminating black vents above and below the firebox) with a traditional look.

In terms of character, the primary drawback to a factory-built fireplace is looks. Most prefabs can't match the enduring charm

This classic French hearth resembles carved stone that is centuries old, but it's actually crafted from stucco.

An antique marble surround is improved by
the addition of old world tiles, actually
reproductions of pieces found in the Vatican.
The iron rail is architectural salvage, stored for
years until the owner found the right use.

{ A PLACE FOR GATHERING 'ROUND, A FIREPLACE PROVIDES SPIRITUAL AS WELL AS PHYSICAL COMFORT. }

of traditional masonry, even when they're lined with paneling that resembles firebrick. A prefab fireplace hardly need be an eyesore, however. The more attention you give to the detailing around a prefab fireplace, the less you'll notice its "manufactured" flavor. Take care in sizing the unit to the surround, so the firebox doesn't look like a tiny hole in a huge hearth, or an overwhelming fire squeezed in a tiny surround.

Take time to shop around and to surf the net—not all factory-made fireplaces are created equal. Metal construction is the norm, but a few companies offer modular units of precast stone and special kit systems that are relatively easy to assemble. With a little legwork and planning, you can create a fireplace with the right blend of charm, convenience, and quality.

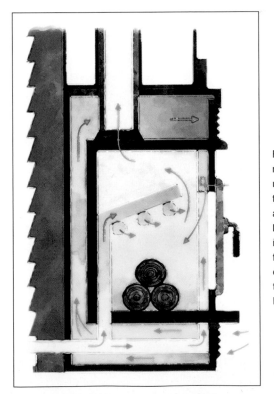

Prefab fireplaces maximize efficiency by using outside air to feed the fire. (Follow the arrows starting at lower left.) Air from the room is circulated around the firebox to heat the inside of the home. (Follow the arrows starting at lower right.)

It may look like classic masonry, but Fido's lounge is a 4-foot-wide manufactured hearth set into a cultured stone wall. The fire isn't old-fashioned, either: It's fueled by gas logs, purchased separately and vented up a chimney.

Seemingly original, this reworked fireplace features a direct-vent gas insert surrounded by new tilework with a running bond pattern. An art-tile chimney accent and vintage sconces complete the makeover.

ADDING A GAS FIREPLACE For many people, a gas fireplace is not simply a cleaner option, it's a better option—easy to install, easy to live with. In locations that include bedrooms and master baths, where convenience and cleanliness are greater priorities, gas fireplaces make even more sense.

Whether the fuel is natural gas or propane, there are three basic types of gas fireplaces: natural-vent, direct-vent, and vent-free. Only the first option—a natural-vent gas fireplace—needs a vertical chimney.

Direct-vent and vent-free gas fireplaces don't need a chimney, and both can double as a heat source. Typically, a direct-vent fireplace is installed next to an exterior wall. Rather than sending exhaust up a chimney, it sends it directly outside through an insulated pipe at the top or back of the unit. The same pipe can bring in fresh air for combustion (it has more than one channel inside). What could be simpler?

To some, the answer to that question is a vent-free fireplace. Highly versatile, these manufactured units can be placed virtually anywhere. They come in a wide array of sizes, shapes, and styles, and can be great for occasional heating. Unfortunately, they also come with a few hitches.

Critics claim that the low-level pollution created by vent-free fireplaces may not be safe for pregnant women or people with respiratory problems. Some states ban these fireplaces altogether. Others prohibit their use in bedrooms. Many locales restrict their use to older construction, because newer homes are much more airtight. If you're interested in a vent-free fireplace, check local codes, size the fireplace to the location, and follow manufacturers' instructions carefully.

{FIREBRICK}

The blonde firebrick (or refractory brick) that lines a firebox doesn't have the look and feel of the brick used to face a fireplace or chimney. The color is lighter, the surface smoother, the edges nice and neat so adjoining bricks can fit together snugly. Modern building codes demand firebrick for a reason: It withstands heat.

INSTALLING A STOVE Efficiency is still the reason many people opt for a freestanding stove instead of a fireplace, but a stove needn't be strictly utilitarian. Many are beautiful in their own right, with intricately detailed doors and gleaming porcelain-enamel skins. Colors range from jewel tones such as ruby, sapphire, and emerald, to classic colors: ivory, white, and ebony. With a broad viewing area in the door, stoves also offer a chance to enjoy the flicker and dance of flames.

You can stoke a stove with logs, but wood isn't your only fuel choice. The same nostalgic look that wood burners offer is available in both direct-vent and vent-free gas models. Pellet-burning stoves are yet another option. Electric models are also available, with "flames" that are surprisingly realistic when you consider they rely on no smoke and a lot of mirrors.

Swedes and Russians have their own favorite way to keep warm: thermal mass heaters. A centuries-old tradition, these are basically a cross between a stove and a wood-burning fireplace. A massive cocoon of soapstone wraps the firebox and rises above it. The stone absorbs heat from the fire, but it stays comfortably warm to the touch, slowly releasing its heat.

If you're considering a cast-iron wood-burning stove, be sure to check the clearance requirements carefully. Most must be installed a certain distance away from walls, and the walls and floors have to be lined with stone or another fireproof material. Gas units are much more flexible.

Opposite: A thick layer of soapstone wraps this Scandinavian-style hearth. The stone soaks up the fire's heat and then slowly releases it, warming a room many hours after the flames have died. Rough and rustic here, soapstone can also be smoothed for a softer, sleeker look.

Left: The glossy finish and fine detail make this metal stove appropriate for even a formal living room. Other stoves have a coarse, cast-iron finish suitable for rustic rooms. Both styles provide plenty of heat.

REMODELING AN EXISTING FIREPLACE

REMODELING AN EXISTING FIREPLACE Plans to upgrade a traditional masonry fireplace should start with a single question: Does it simply need a facelift, or are there functional problems as well? If the latter is true, you may want to add a fireplace insert—a manufactured gas or wood-burning unit that slips inside your existing firebox. (A new chimney liner may also be required.) So before you begin any makeover, it's best to have the fireplace and chimney inspected for problems, such as cracks in the flue, and to discuss any proposed changes with a qualified professional who understands your situation and local building codes.

Stylistically, options for upgrading a fireplace are virtually limitless. As in any makeover, success comes from choosing a look that fits the overall style of your home as well as the scale and formality of the surrounding room. Also consider furniture placement, and the activities that will take place in the room.

Sometimes, all a tired brick fireplace needs is a new mantel and a fresh coat of paint. It's also possible to remove paint from stone or brick through sandblasting, but that's a messy and expensive proposition, worthwhile only if you're sure

Above and opposite: A bold take on classic, this fireplace was designed by the architect as part of a remodeling, and updates a formerly dark and somber room. The slip and hearth are limestone, surrounded by a painted wood mantel. A flat panel adorned with fins arches over the firebox to join a pair of wedge-shape capitals. Inexpensive copper plumbing caps bejewel the shelf front, punctuating each support.

{BEFORE}

A classic white mantel frames a spectacle of falling leaves. Dismayed by the drab fireplace in their 1980s tract house, the owners chiseled away the old surround and started over. Sand-color grout secures the leaves, each of which is an elegant, handcrafted tile. Tumbled marble tile covers the hearth, while dentil molding and a narrow rope detail accent the painted wood shelf.

you'll find a wonderful surface below. In older homes, a more beautiful chimney or fireplace may be lurking behind an ill-conceived cover-up of paneling or plaster.

More often, however, a cover-up is what's needed—one that makes the original fireplace disappear. You might decide to add a new or salvaged mantelpiece, as well as a new slip. Wood panels and moldings are the classic treatment, but mantels can also be made of carved or cast stone, synthetic stone, or even metal. Or you can cover an entire surround with stone veneer—from slabs of granite or marble to man-made river rock. For a classic or contemporary look, choose smooth, polished stone. For a more rustic take, leave it rough or honed. Though you may find adequate materials at a local home improvement store, you're cheating yourself if you don't at least explore the wider possibilities.

Tile—ceramic, stone, or art tile—is another cover-up option. Art tile or glass and metal mosaics can be stunning

but pricey. If you can't afford an entire surround using your favorite art tile, consider a smaller grouping of well-placed accents. Stone tiles are usually more affordable and easier to install than solid slabs. Slate, often relatively inexpensive, comes in a range of hues, from gray to golden to green. Granite offers a more dizzying array of colors and patterns, including varieties that reveal secondary colors like sweet surprises when viewed at an angle. Remember that slate and marble are relatively porous and prone to staining if left unsealed. Granite is denser, so it's less likely to stain.

A final note: If you're weary of burning wood but think your masonry fireplace looks just fine, consider adding gas logs (a gas line and a ceramic log set) to the firebox. You'll send a good deal of the heat up the chimney, but this is the least expensive way to convert to gas, and it lets you retain the traditional look of your fireplace

Left: It looks massive, but this 6-foot-wide fireplace owes its beauty to a limestone veneer, which conceals a plain brick fireplace. The brick had been already covered once before: It was discovered beneath ugly wood paneling and a marble slip. An arch above the firebox and projecting stones below the mantelpiece reflect the work of a skilled mason.

Opposite: Curious about concrete, two contractors created this naturalistic surround for their home. After tearing off the old mantel, they built and filled three frames in their basement (two concrete supports and a lintel), then pressed leaves into the surface. Strong adhesive secures panels to the underlying brick.

{BEFORE}

{BEFORE}

{FLAME AND FASHION}

Above: Modern fireplace styles have sleek lines and smooth surfaces, but the most pleasing hearths still have echoes of the fireplace's traditional styling. Note the streamlined classic mantel here. The polished stone hearth reflects the fire's energetic flames.

Upper right: The rustic setting of this room is well-suited to the traditional deep brick firebox of this hearth. The generous size of this fireplace reflects its practical history.

Right: The joy of modern engineering means you can have any mantel style with all the conveniences, such as this two-sided gas fireplace wrapped with an elaborate surround.

A SPARK IN TIME

Fireplaces have always been important stylistically, setting the tone for everything else in a room. If you're renovating an older home—or just hoping to make a new house feel old—you might want to do a little research on which styles were prevalent during your favorite period. Here's a quick rundown of fireplace fashions from the past few centuries:

1500-1625

Tudor and Jacobean. During the Tudor and Jacobean periods in Britain, hearths were grandly scaled with broad lintels spanning cavernous openings. Mantelpiece designs were as elaborate as any you might find in a church.

1795-1850

Neoclassic. During the late 1700s and early 1800s, designers looked to Greece and Rome. Wooden surrounds and overmantels featured a great deal of finery. Homeowners who could afford a solid marble surround often embraced simpler designs with less ornamentation. Others settled for marble slips and gussied up the woodwork.

1860-1920

Arts and Crafts. Arts and Crafts fireplaces featured clean, simple lines and spare geometry. But not everything was rectilinear. Sinewy vines, stylized leaves and flowers, elegant long-tailed birds—all appeared during the Arts and Crafts era, in art-tile accents, as well as mantels made of beaten copper and cast iron.

1910-1940

Art Deco. One thing can always be said about Art Deco: It made waves! Popular motifs—such as wavy borders and "stepping" patterns—made their way into fireplace designs during this period.

1600-1775

1715-1840

Georgian. During the early Georgian period (the early 1700s), fashionable Europeans ordered elaborately carved mantels and paired them with marble slips. Classical designs— wave patterns, scrolling acanthus leaves, Ionic pilasters at the sides— gave mantels added grace.

Colonial American. In early Colonial America, it was common to forgo the overmantel and hang a large painting above the fireplace. Wall paneling often surrounded the entire fireplace, framing it like a showpiece.

1830-1905

Victorian. Victorians had no fear of ornamentation, either—though their fireplace designs frequently took a more Gothic turn and embraced medieval European traditions. Built-in cabinetry, raised paneling, elaborate overmantels with spindles and fretwork—any or all of these might be gathered around the hearth to underscore its importance.

1920-1960

1950-1970

American Modernism. The operative word for American Modernism is sleek. Look for long, lean lines with few adornments. Some fireplaces in this style don't even have mantels.

Prairie Style. Frank Lloyd Wright, the prominent architect when this style first appeared, often included a central fireplace, dividing rooms in what was then a daringly open plan. Plainspoken natural materials adds to the earthy quality of these homes.

Framed by handsome built-ins, this Craftsman-style fireplace is another clever cover-up. Harlequin tile and a crisp white mantel conceal the original hearth. An arch above the firebox echoes the curve of the gas fireplace insert.

Reminiscent of Rookwood pottery, unglazed field tile and hand-painted accents add character to a gas fireplace. Twig-look border tile underlines the mantel.

THE MORE ATTENTION YOU GIVE TO THE DETAILING AROUND A PREFABRICATED FIREPLACE, THE LESS YOU'LL NOTICE ITS "MANUFACTURED" FLAVOR.

Left: A tumbled slate hearth meets simulated limestone in this earthy pairing. The limestone stretches from floor to ceiling, with a simple oak beam (not shown) serving as the mantel.

Below: A carefully planned tile layout is reflected in this stunning centerpiece, which features a circular vine relief. A raised hearth provides extra seating and adds a gentle curve to the design.

Strips of recycled fir flooring form a graceful trim line above this fireplace, mimicking the arch of the firebox below.

A fresh take on Pueblo style, a massive stone fireplace with a raised hearth and a granite slip reflects the colors and textures of the desert. Cutouts in the surrounding built-ins recall the pictograms of early Native American cultures.

{STAIRWAYS}

Few interior elements rival the
sculptural beauty and visual
impact of a well-designed flight
of stairs. Architects have long seen
them as an opportunity to add
drama to a home, especially the
stairs in a foyer. Prominently
positioned, they make an opening
statement about the character
and quality of a house and the
personalities of those live within it.

Opposite: Niches, a built-in bench, and a dramatic overlook distinguish this winding central stairway. Coffee-color stair nosing, wall-caps, and railings create rhythmic, horizontal lines.

Left: The centerpiece in a split-level home's makeover, this stairway features a neoclassic balustrade inspired by a historical pattern. The handsome newel post complements paneled wainscoting, which descends into the foyer. Note the three-part front door with fixed sides; its generous proportions match the wide stairway.

TYPES OF STAIRS Whether you're planning an addition that includes a new stairway or considering a makeover for the stairs you already have, it's a good idea to become familiar with stairway configurations. Here are some popular examples:

A straight-run stair, as the name suggests, creates a direct path from one floor to the next in a single flight, without a turn. It's the least expensive type of stair to build and consumes relatively little floor space.

A dogleg stair has two straight flights that run in different directions, with a broad landing between them. (Some designers call this a scissor stair, because the two flights resemble the blades in a pair of open scissors.)

A quarter-turn dogleg with a flare offers the flavor of a curved stair at a lower cost and within a tighter space. The first flight "flares" out gracefully on one or both sides.

A curved stair is the epitome of elegance. For even more drama, some curved stairs are freestanding—cantilevered with no wall below.

A winder stair makes directional changes without a landing or platform. Instead, it incorporates a series of winder treads at the turn (treads that are wedge-shape instead of rectangular). Because the rise continues at the turn, this kind of stair demands a little less space than a dogleg stair.

Spiral stairs form a circle, revolving around a single newel or pole. They're the most space-efficient type of stair, but they're also the least comfortable to climb. Carrying furniture up a tight spiral stair is, at best, a challenge.

Opposite: Simple and elegant, the wrought iron balusters on this stairway attach to the stringer rather than sprouting from the treads. Note how this co completely changes the look of the staircase.

Above: A menagerie of sea creatures rides the graceful swell of this custom-made iron balustrade. Twisted balusters alternate with those sporting crown-shape flourishes.

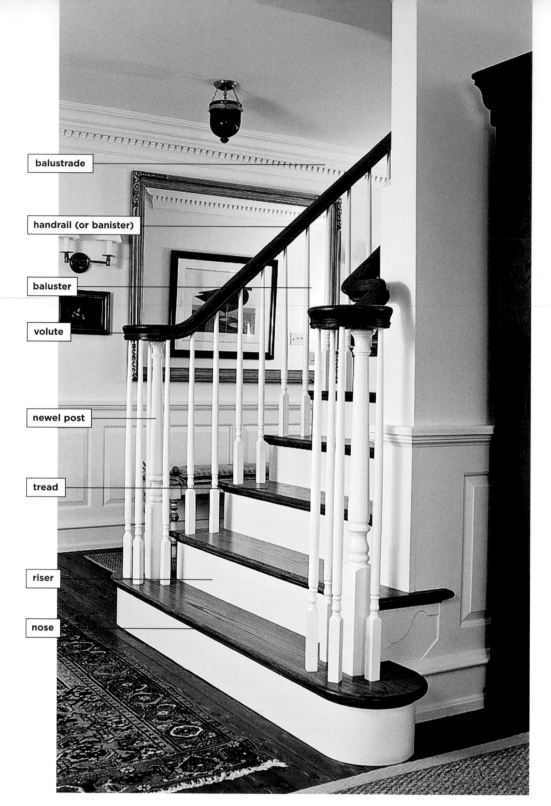

balustrade

handrail (or banister)

baluster

volute

newel post

tread

riser

nose

ANATOMY OF A STAIR

Every stairway includes the same basic elements. The style is determined largely by the material and shaping of each part. Here's a quick tour of a stairway's anatomy and the decorative twists you might find along the way:

The tread is the horizontal part of the stair you step on. Between each one is the **riser**, which is vertical. The sizing of these parts is very important: It determines a stairway's rise, or steepness, a measurement that is tightly controlled by building codes.

Classic millwork gives this quarter-turn stairway its casual grace. Square balusters march in threes past a built-in bench that hides galoshes. Subtle wall framing wraps a lighted niche at the journey's start (far right), as well as its end (upstairs, not shown). An under-stair cabinet displays family photos and treasures.

The nose is the front edge of a tread. Often it's rounded, with a strip of cove molding below to ease the transition back to the riser.

A stringer is a board that stretches diagonally along the sides of a stairway. In an open stair with a closed-string design, the stringer covers the edge of the treads, so you see a diagonal line stretching along the rise, instead of a zigzagging or "stepping" line. The balusters are usually anchored to a shallow "wall" instead of resting on the treads.

When a stairway has an open-string design, you can see the stepped profile of the treads and risers from the side. Each tread has a return (a finished edge facing the side). This design also reveals the tread ends: the wedge-shape area at the side of a stair nestled between the tread and riser.

The balustrade is the entire railing assembly and often the true measure of the stairmaker's artistry. It includes the top rail (banister or handrail), the individual spindles (balusters), and usually a bottom rail as well. It also includes the newels, the upright posts that link each section of railing. The starting newel is often turned and carved to create an auspicious beginning. Here the railing may curve into a nautiluslike scroll, or volute, or be topped with a distinctive finial. A box newel is a large, stout, square post, protruding above the railing. Its surfaces may be plain or adorned with carvings and moldings, and the interior is often hollow.

In a post-to-post railing design, the newels interrupt the railing. A continuous or over-the-post railing is a more sensuous (and expensive) arrangement: You can slide your fingers down the entire length of the railing without having to raise your hand.

Opposite left: This lovely trellis-style balustrade may not be permissible under some building codes, which commonly restrict openings to 4 inches or less.

Opposite right: Cutouts embellish a plank-style balustrade in a sunny Swedish decor. Design possibilities for such cutouts are virtually limitless.

Left: Discovered beneath a casing of cheap paneling and wallboard in a Victorian cottage, this charming balustrade includes scrolled panels and an extra-stout newel post with notches and rosettes.

Above: A curved, expanded first step makes the start of a stairway more special and noticeable.

IMPROVING A STAIR If your stairway isn't living up to its potential, improve it. A successful makeover can be as simple as painting or refinishing the existing woodwork or as complex as bumping out a stairwell. In between, you'll find options such as these:

Open it up. A light-filled, open stairway is pleasing to climb and descend. An enclosed stair feels more like a tunnel.

Improve the views. Look for opportunities to add a special window along the stairway. If you have an existing window with an unpleasant view, obscure it with art glass, so the natural light is preserved. If the stairway doesn't border an outside wall, consider adding a skylight or clerestory window overhead.

You can create a more dramatic beginning by expanding the starting step and inserting a more elegant boxed newel post.

Change the balustrade. A balustrade offers the chance for personal expression, allowing you to introduce a symbol or motif that's meaningful and pleasing to you.

Upgrade materials. If your current stairs are plywood topped with carpet, and hardwood treads and risers are too costly, consider a hybrid step: The center of each step remains plywood, while special hardwood veneer covers the rest Then a runner of carpeting is secured over the middle of the steps.

Add built-ins. Tuck a settee at the base of the stairs. A generous landing space can become a small gallery or library with the addition of built-ins for displaying treasures or books. If there's a view, install a window seat.

Change the entire stair. It's a bold move, but not impossible. You can have a new stair built on-site, or order the entire stairway preassembled, with minimal remodeling fuss.

A note of caution: Local building codes often restrict the changes you make, so be sure to check codes before changing any structure, including the railing.

{UPGRADING A BASEMENT STAIR}

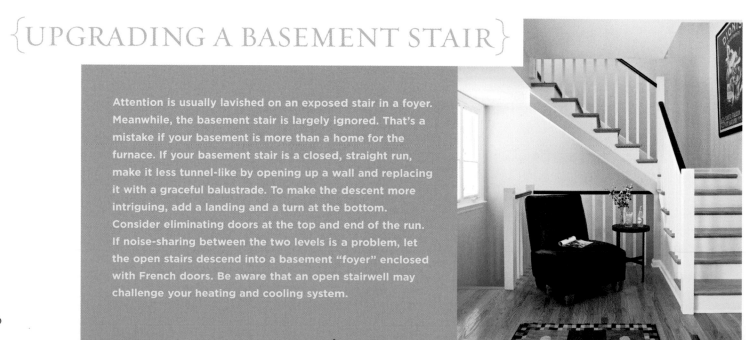

Attention is usually lavished on an exposed stair in a foyer. Meanwhile, the basement stair is largely ignored. That's a mistake if your basement is more than a home for the furnace. If your basement stair is a closed, straight run, make it less tunnel-like by opening up a wall and replacing it with a graceful balustrade. To make the descent more intriguing, add a landing and a turn at the bottom. Consider eliminating doors at the top and end of the run. If noise-sharing between the two levels is a problem, let the open stairs descend into a basement "foyer" enclosed with French doors. Be aware that an open stairwell may challenge your heating and cooling system.

Right: This stairway's classical urn-style finial was inspired by a fence post. Note the wavelike pattern adorning the tread ends. Such pieces can be purchased separately from a millwork specialist.

Above: A nightlight encased in stained glass makes this newel post an alluring safety feature after bedtime.

Left: A balustrade of wood and steel with metal cables accentuates the long, lean lines of this contemporary home.

91

{BUILT-INS}

A cozy window seat. A colonial corner cupboard. A Swedish-style bed snuggled below sloping eaves. Built-in furnishings have a romantic appeal, and while we can't take them with us when we move, the best examples are as cherished as freestanding heirlooms.

Like many of the elements that give a home character, they represent the union of form and function. They should be beautiful, but they must also be useful, adding both comfort and style to a home. Built-in furniture makes highly efficient use of a small space. Cabinets and built-in shelving provide storage for the stuff of life, hiding messes and organizing necessities while putting treasures on display. Added to a room that's grand and empty, built-ins can even reshape its boundaries, creating alcoves and curving vestibules for a cost that's well below the expense of a traditional bump-out.

These playful family-room built-ins represent budget-minded beauty. Framing and drywall form much of the structure, replacing costlier hardwoods.

Mimicking the stairway's climb, these built-in cabinets use space that might otherwise be wasted. Mullioned glass doors complement the home's casual cottage style.

Though built-ins grace interiors of virtually every era, they're especially common in Prairie-style homes. Frank Lloyd Wright used built-ins to define spaces in otherwise open floor plans and determine the finished look of interiors. (He had little patience for homeowners who muddled up his designs with inappropriate decor.) To Wright, a home's interior details were a natural extension of its exterior architecture. It is "quite impossible" to consider a building and its furnishings as separate entities, he once noted.

When you're contemplating new built-ins, remember that permanence is a double-edged sword. Freestanding furniture can be changed at a whim, but built-ins are a long-term commitment, so it's all the more important that they be thoughtfully designed and well-crafted. A high-quality built-in gives a house greater substance, but an ugly or shabby one just detracts from a home's character.

Style is an issue as well. While you might take an eclectic approach to other furnishings—mixing 1950s modern with 18th-century antiques, for instance— built-ins look best when they merge seamlessly with a home's existing architectural details, especially its woodwork and trim.

Opposite top left: Nestled in an arched niche, a built-in sideboard enhances a contemporary dining room. Recessed lighting in the curved soffit softly washes the wall with light.

Opposite below left: A tale of beauty and beasts, these kitchen built-ins include denlike nooks for snoozing pooches. Another pet-friendly touch (not shown): floor-level niches to keep water and food bowls clear of traffic.

Opposite below right: A built-in bench flanked by leaded-glass cabinets welcomes guests to this Arts and Crafts-style foyer. A possible variation: Convert the cabinets to coat storage.

Left: Sleek anigre wood cabinets hold a TV and family photos in this contemporary living room. Cabinet doors below and beside the TV spring open with a gentle push.

SITTING PRETTY A bay window is a natural spot for a window seat, but virtually any window is a candidate, especially when surrounding built-ins create a niche. Stretched languidly below a gang of windows, a broad seat invites afternoon catnaps. Here are some guidelines for sizing up the possibilities:

Height: Most seats are between 16 and 20 inches above the floor. Ideally, they should be lower than the windowsill—at least 6 inches lower if you're adding throw pillows or a backrest. Allow 2 to 4 inches of thickness for a standard seat cushion. (Have foam cut to fit,

then upholster it.) Consider window hardware too: Cranks may impinge on the seat.

Depth: Common depths (front to back) are between 12 and 36 inches, but the ideal measurement depends on your floor space and surrounding built-ins. Allow 1 foot for a child, and 2 feet for an adult using a back pillow. For occasional naps, a 3-foot depth is comfortable.

Length: Do some field-testing in preferred positions. If you'd like to recline while reading a book, a 6-foot-long seat is usually adequate. Add a few more inches and a deep window seat can double as a bed for overnight guests.

Opposite: This under-stair cubby is a perfect spot for a child to tie on tennies or curl up with a storybook. An unexpected window captures a special woodland view.

Left: Tall cabinets embrace this corner window seat, which is crafted of cherry wood. The generously sized bench lets readers recline, provides extra seating, and accommodates two sleeping children.

THE BEST BANQUETTES

Inviting and space-efficient, a built-in banquette take up less room than a traditional table because you don't have to wrestle with chairs. Designing the ideal banquette is a matter of finding—or creating—the perfect nook. Almost any spot is a candidate, says San Francisco designer Denise Sheldon. "I've put [dining niches] in corners, bay windows, all kinds of odd spaces." In her hands, a little 6x7-foot nook can become a plush retreat for six. Here are her tips:

Size things up carefully. Allow about 2 linear feet per person for bench seating. Benches are typically 16 inches deep. Tables can be as narrow as 28 inches for two people.

Seize opportunities. Add built-in shelving above a banquette and bench storage below. Because the niche feels like a special room, it can handle a special treatment. "It's the one place in the kitchen you can decorate, hang a wonderful chandelier, or use wild wallpaper," Sheldon says.

Above left: More comfortable than the tangle of chairs it replaced, this L-shape banquette handles everything from breakfast to homework. Throw pillows cushion the slanted backrest.

Left: A shapely banquette throws a curve into a boxy plan, making the most of a tight corner. The back of the bench provides shelf space.

Built-ins transformed a blank wall into this congenial niche at the edge of the cooking zone in this open kitchen. Arched niches flank the bench, repeating a curved valance.

99

SHAPING SPACE Walls and half walls typically define or shape a room, but built-ins can do the job as well. Consider these options:

Add curve appeal. Sensuously curved built-ins offer visual relief from boxy plans. A long window seat shaped into a crescent softens the edges of a rectangular room. Built-ins around a doorway can be sculpted so they curve inward next to the passage, adding grace and drama to the entrance.

Find your niche. Instead of bumping out, "bump in" with built-ins—achieving a similar look without a costly remodeling of exterior walls. A bench or window seat is a classic use of such a niche, but a desk or vanity could feel equally at ease nestled between built-in bookshelves. With its headboard surrounded by tall shelving or cabinetry, a freestanding bed becomes a sheltered retreat. (Leave room for bedside tables, or build them in as well, adding thoughtfully integrated wall lamps.)

Define boundaries. Like half walls, built-ins can serve as room dividers in an otherwise open plan, while putting new "wall" space to work.

Right: Shape and color set this curved cabinet apart from the rest of the kitchen. Though not an antique, it adds old-world character while softening the room's sharp angles.

Opposite: Both a storage wall and a style statement, these floor-to-ceiling built-ins share views between adjacent rooms. Integrated spotlights shine upon lofty treasures.

{ LIKE MANY ELEMENTS OF CHARACTER, BUILT-INS REPRESENT THE UNION OF FORM AND FUNCTION—OF BEAUTY AND COMFORT. }

Above: A well-planned wall of bedroom built-ins keeps clothing neat and accessible while consuming far less floor space than a traditional closet.

Right: Nestled beneath a window, a child's built-in bed is equally inviting day or night. Drawer pulls from boat cleats complement the room's nautical theme.

Below: Tall closets create a niche for a window seat in this charming bedroom. By painting the unit white, it stands out boldly and emphasizes the sunny side of the room.

SPACES

A critical step in understanding what gives a home character is examining how we react to certain spaces. What makes us feel good?

It's more than a matter of style. A character-rich home is filled with special touches, but it doesn't have to be fancy. Being impressed by a space is not the same thing as feeling comfortable there. This chapter helps you identify the spatial qualities that enrich the flavor of a home, filling it with comfort at every turn while creating an overall sense of harmony.

{CONNECTIONS}

The character of a room is shaped by its relationship to the spaces around it. When designing a home, architects pay careful attention to the *sight lines*—how far the eye travels from point A to point B and where it rests between. Long sight lines are almost always desirable; the farther you can see, the larger and more interesting a sequence of rooms begins to feel. Within a rectangle, the longest line is the diagonal, so opening up the views along this axis is a good way to make a small room feel larger.

Two passages can be better than one. A new doorway on the left improves connections between this Craftsman-style dining room and the remodeled kitchen and family room beyond. Open transoms and elegant trimwork complete the makeover.

INVITING VIEWS Consider opening things up. A long, straight sight line that stretches from room to room and ultimately leads to a sunlit garden view helps a house live beyond its boundaries. Aligning the passages and openings along the way can emphasize the ultimate destination and create a reassuring sense of order.

Teasing views—partial glimpses of the space beyond—are equally important to the character of a home. Like a bend in the road, they invite us to explore, promising hints of adventure. When our efforts are rewarded with pleasant waysides, an entire house can become a journey that we're glad to take again and again.

OPEN SPACES, SEPARATE PLACES Not so long ago, most homes were a collection of very discrete rooms. Kitchens were small and isolated.

Today open plans are in high demand. But even though the connections between rooms are stronger, we still crave a variety of spaces. A comfortable home strikes a pleasing balance, offering a mix of private and public rooms, and spaces that are both cozy and large.

It also offers certain well-defined spaces with a natural sequence and flow. For our guests, we want an inviting and welcoming entry that creates a graceful transition between the outside world and more private realms. For ourselves, we appreciate a practical mudroom to corral outerwear, school gear, and mail. From here, the kitchen can't be far, because this is the path that groceries take to the fridge. The kitchen, in turn, is the heart of the home, surrounded by the casual living and dining areas.

Right: A nod to 1940s nostalgia, a telephone niche is a fitting focal point for a remodeled front hall. Matching archways create visual rhythm.

Right center and bottom: "Bumping in" is a cost-effective alternative to bumping out. Crafted mostly from standard framing and drywall, an arched niche serves as an intimate reading nook and an architectural focal point. Well-planned storage offers shelving for books, a resting spot for teacups, and electrical outlets for lighting. Cubbies below the bench maximize storage with baskets for reading materials and covers.

Above: A floor-level change and a broad passage delineate this family room from an eat-in kitchen, sharing views while preserving a separate identity for each space. An added bonus: a lowered floor allows the family room ceiling to soar.

ALCOVES AND NOOKS When we're shaping a comfortable space for living, humans universally crave two sides of the same coin: We want containment as well as freedom, shelter as well as openness.

Think about the spaces you already have. Would it be possible to sculpt a small sitting area using built-ins? How might a bump-out enhance the look and function of an existing room? If the room is already large, you also might create a cozy nook by lowering the ceiling height over a section at the edge. (As an added bonus, the rest of the ceiling will seem higher by comparison.)

A nook or alcove can be an extremely efficient use of space, but achieving true comfort takes careful planning— knowing how and when you will actually *use* this little refuge and ensuring that you size and finish it accordingly.

Above: To make room for a massive fireplace and inglenook, homeowners added a 6-foot bumpout. A structural beam and columns make the hearth an even grander focal point.

Left: Long sight lines that stretch to the outdoors help any house live larger. The final opening in this scene isn't perfectly aligned, but each passage frames a carefully balanced composition. Teasing views of the rooms along the way invite exploration.

Well-trimmed built-ins add depth to this paneled passageway, making the walls seem more substantial. Curved niches above the cabinets repeat the central arch.

{ DRAMA OVERHEAD }

Gazing at a floor plan, we can readily gauge the square footage and basic shape of a room, but we can't judge the quality of a space unless we know what's happening overhead. Topped by a flat 8-foot-high ceiling, a 14×14-foot family room may feel cramped. But if the ceiling vaults even a few feet higher, the character of the room improves. Add generous windows or French doors, and it can feel downright voluminous.

A series of arched, laminated beams support this dramatic barrel-vault ceiling, warmed by slender planks of Douglas fir. Custom transoms echo the curve and capture a slice of the sky.

A coved ceiling lends understated elegance to this clean-lined space. Largely a cosmetic treatment, the upgrade required no change to the overlying structure. Uplights tucked atop the soffit add nighttime glow.

When every ceiling in a house follows the same never-ending plane, the overall effect is pretty dull, even if the ceilings are uniformly high. Special places call for special treatments. Varying the height and shape of an important ceiling can add considerable drama to a room. A distinctive ceiling is powerful enough that it defines the space below it—even when that space has no walls to suggest its boundaries.

The following is a brief survey of the ways an existing ceiling can be lifted or sculpted to improve the character of a room. (For a decorative trim treatment that can dress up a ceiling, see the Appendix.)

Cathedral ceilings. A cathedral, or vaulted, ceiling soars to a home's roofline, closely following its pitch. Unless the joists

in the attic floor remain intact, a ceiling of this type requires special construction.

Shed ceilings (flounders). A variation on a cathedral ceiling, this is what happens when a roof ridge is above a room's wall. Instead of a central peak, the ceiling rises to one side, like a shed roof.

Tray ceilings. Easier to construct than a cathedral ceiling, a tray ceiling has angled soffits around the perimeter, which rise to a high, flat ceiling in the center space. Among the variations: A *two-sided tray* has only two sloped sides, on opposite sides of the room. A *stepped tray* climbs to a recessed area in the center of the ceiling using two or three right-angle steps, which resemble the underside of an open stairway.

Coved ceilings. Traditionally, a coved ceiling meets each wall with a graceful curve. But this term has also come to refer to a lowered shelf-style soffit that edges the perimeter of the room, especially when soft lighting tucks above it. By offering a contrast in height, the soffit makes the center area of the ceiling feel loftier, even though it hasn't risen at all. Because they seldom involve structural changes, coved ceilings are relatively easy to create.

Above: A double-recess lends drama and breathing room to an 8-foot ceiling, transforming a formerly dull, boxy little bedroom. A stylish ceiling fan punctuates the visual statement.

Right: It looks lofty, but this sunroom's vaulted ceiling matches the shallow roof of a ranch-style home. Peek-through gables offer treetop views and enhance the sense of height. Green-painted planks ground the space while strengthening ties to the landscape.

A series of pendants adds panache to overhead beams and draws the eye downward, giving the room a cozier scale. Pale painted woodwork suits the room's casual cottage flavor.

Barrel vaults or curves. An arched ceiling that echoes the shape of a half barrel is called a barrel vault. As long as you work below existing joists, creating similar curves overhead may be easier than you think. And you're not limited to vaults; curved soffits are another design option. Imagine creating a half-moon alcove at the edge of a boxy room, defined by a curved soffit overhead and a matching built-in bench below.

Recessed ceilings. If your attic space is accessible, you can often reframe a section of the ceiling to create a recessed area overhead. The effect is similar to what you'd get by adding a lower soffit along the edges, except you're actually boosting the ceiling height.

An octagonal kitchen addition is greatly enhanced by a sculpted ceiling that follows the rooflines. Scooped into one of the facets, a custom window creates a focal point above the sink.

{WINDOWS}

In a traditional colonial house, expansive views are best created by gangs of windows or matching doors with small divisions. Only one of these doors opens; the rest are fixed.

Thoughtfully placed, a specialty window can offer a visual surprise or make a grand impression. This round window does both. Facing a side yard, it brightens the foyer of a once-drab cottage, signaling the home's new, improved personality.

An upgrade for a 1950s ranch, stacked transoms transform this breakfast nook into a contemporary sunroom. Awning-style crank-outs at the bottom admit breezes.

We celebrate homes bathed in light, but we don't always live in them. Upgrading windows is one of the easiest ways to enhance a home's character short of a major remodeling, offering both style and comfort in a single package.

TYPES OF WINDOWS Windows come in five basic designs. The difference literally hinges on function, because it's the way the windows open and close that distinguishes each group.

Double-hung windows have two sashes that move up and down, sliding past one another in the same track. *Single-hung* windows look similar, but only one sash moves.

Casement windows swing or crank out from side hinges, much like doors. It's important to

Paired with French doors, a Juliette balcony matches the appeal of the real thing—without the cost of extending a platform outside. An arched soffit adds interest and depth to the room.

Fixed windows don't open at all. Without moving parts, they're cheaper to produce, so they often line up as economical "look-alikes" in a gang of windows where only partial ventilation is required.

Other examples hail from the exotic realm of specialty windows. Distinguished by their dramatic shapes (and higher prices), these include anything from an octagonal window that accents a high gable to an arched transom that tops a French door.

ELEMENTS OF STYLE Look closely at a house whose character you admire. Windows play a major role in establishing its architectural style—both inside and out. A cozy Cape Cod or a stately Colonial just wouldn't feel right without double-hung windows. Casement windows have a much longer history, which makes them just as appropriate to storybook English cottages as they are to Spanish casitas and high-style examples from the Prairie School.

But design type is not the only element that determines a window's personality. In fact, how a window opens is seldom as important as the way it's trimmed, shaped, and divided. Not all windows are rectangles. In a Mission-style home, for instance, you might find a pair of casements whose curved tops form a shallow arch when they meet. Fanlights (arched, fixed windows topping others) are popular on Federal-style homes, especially above the front door. Proportions matter too—from the beefiness of the bottom rail to whether a window's overall shape is tall and slim or relatively broad.

You can dramatically change the style of any window simply by adding *muntins*—slender moldings that partition a sash into multiple windowpanes. The patterns are distinctive and they're often associated with particular styles of architecture. The tall double-hung windows on a Queen Anne are often "two-over-two," for instance, with both the upper and lower

account for the swing if you add these windows while remodeling, ensuring that the windows can open freely and won't become head-banging hazards above a narrow sidewalk, for instance.

Awning windows are hinged at the top, swinging open at the bottom. Seated atop other windows they become transoms, but just about any position is possible.

Sliders move from side to side in a track. They're particularly useful in a tight spot—overlooking a small back porch, for instance—and can be styled to match casements that appear elsewhere.

Slender divided casements and matching French doors suit the understated elegance of an updated Mediterranean-style home.

Top above: Protected from the elements, a salvaged antique window shares light between interior rooms.

Above: This oval window is a fabulous, hand-painted fake, accenting a high gable.

Sometimes the character of a room is shaped by its ties to the surrounding landscape. Here a small suburban lot has become a private oasis that extends into the adjacent dining room via almost-floor-to-ceiling-glass French doors.

HOW A WINDOW OPENS IS SELDOM AS
IMPORTANT TO ITS STYLE AS THE WAY
IT IS TRIMMED, SHAPED, AND DIVIDED.

sashes divided by a vertical bar. On Georgian homes, "six-over-six" double-hungs prevail, while many Shingle-style homes have "eight-over-ones." On a Craftsman bungalow, you'll often find double-hungs with an open sash below and four vertical divisions above.

Opposite: Casement windows with diagonal panes are appropriate to Tudor-style homes as well as high-style houses from the Prairie School.

Above: Set in a front-facing gable, a stunning arch-top window echoes the ceiling's gracefully curved edges. Style like this was once commonplace, even in humble cottages.

The way in which windows are grouped also impacts the look and flavor of a home. On a Georgian manor, single windows march across the front facade with perfect rhythm and symmetry. On a Tudor-style home, the windows often mingle in groups of three, while Prairie-style windows gang together to form light-loving ribbons of glass.

With so many elements in play, choosing the ideal windows for a house may seem a little daunting. If you're ready for a change, ask an architect or designer to help you choose a look that best complements the style of your house.

Prairie-style glass doors reflect the style of six-over-one windows by repeating the pattern of their uppermost panes. Well-tailored trim and a turn in the wall camouflage the disparity between door and window heights.

DESIGNING WITH WINDOWS Whether you're adding one window to your home or an entire houseful, here are a few design guidelines that will help ensure a successful result:

Be consistent. This fundamental rule applies no less to windows than to any other stylistic feature in your home. New windows should match or complement the style of the originals—unless you plan to change them throughout the house.

Consider the view. When a room opens up to a beautiful view, its character changes dramatically and it seems much larger than before. If you don't have a view, create one by drawing the eye to focal points in a revamped landscape.

Plan for privacy. When privacy is a concern—or a view can't be improved—install windows that welcome light while obscuring the scenery with frosted panes or colored art glass.

Shutter-style casements open to a wrought-iron railing with a planter box, capturing the flavor of an old-world balcony.

You also can capture considerable light with high transoms or gable windows.

Seek a balanced light. Every exposure—east, west, north, or south—creates a different light and mood. North, for instance, has cool tones and a soft, even quality. Western exposures can be harsh in summer, but offer dramatic sunset views. The ideal choice includes at least two exposure for a room; the preference is three.

{VARIATIONS ON A THEME}

All windows offer connections to the outdoors, but the following options take us a step further—either by projecting into the garden or providing a passageway that gets us there.

Bays and bows. No ordinary window can match the sense of spaciousness that a bay or bow window brings to a room. What's the difference between a bay and a bow? A bay has two angled sides, while a bow approximates a curve (without actually having curved windows). Note that a traditional angled bay with 45-degree sides isn't right for every home. In a contemporary setting, for instance, a box bay with 90-degree sides may be more appropriate.

Glass doors. French doors should be styled to complement your window array. If you have no room for the doors' swing, consider a slider. They've come a long way since they debuted in the 1950s.

Line it up. Each wall of your home forms a two-dimensional composition—just like a painting or drawing. As a general rule, the tops of windows (header heights) on any given level should line up precisely. The bottoms (sill heights) can vary, stretching closer to or farther from the floor. But if the header height goes up and down, everything feels off-kilter.

That doesn't mean windows can never climb above the header height. You might want to add glass to a gable to accent a vaulted ceiling, or place transoms atop other windows in a sunroom. The key is to start with windows that match the prevailing header height, and then add more above them. The line between the two sections becomes a reference point that creates a more harmonious composition.

Study proportions. The ratio of a window's width to its height—its basic proportion—is an important element of design. Even when window sizes vary, you often can create a sense of unity by keeping the relative proportions the same.

Remember the furniture. Before you install any new window, think about how you'll use the space. If furnishings float away from the walls, window size may be irrelevant. But if you need to position a couch or table below a window, be sure the sill is high enough to accommodate it.

REPLACEMENT STRATEGIES A replacement window is the no-fuss option for anyone who'd like to replace windows with more energy-efficient versions or multipaned sashes without changing the size of the openings. Everything around the window can stay in place, including the trim. The new sash slips right into place.

French doors aren't only for exteriors. These carefully aligned passages separate a master suite's dressing area from the bath beyond, allowing light and views to flow.

{ WHEN A ROOM OPENS UP TO A BEAUTIFUL
VIEW, ITS CHARACTER CHANGES DRAMATICALLY,
AND IT SEEMS MUCH LARGER THAN BEFORE. }

INTERIOR LIGHTING

Optimists at heart, we plan our homes as if the sun always shines, relishing a space that is bathed in light. But what happens after nightfall? Or on a cloudy day? Artificial lighting is just as important to the mood and character of your house as its natural counterpart. And like the sun and sky, it can be changeable—only this time, the mood and level of brightness are within your control. A successful lighting scheme can reshape your interior world, accentuating its strengths and blurring its weaknesses, all while adding depth and dimension to your home.

Artificial lighting shapes the mood and character of a space. But when it comes to lighting our homes, we often settle for far less than what is possible. As long as we have sufficient light to see, and the effect isn't unbearably harsh or glaring, we tend to accept it. Or we focus on the style of a fixture— the rustic sconce, the trendy table lamp—and forget that its primary purpose is illumination.

{THE POWER OF LIGHT}

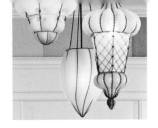

Not surprisingly, lighting designers have an entirely different attitude. To them, lighting is a science that encompasses physics, geometry, and electrical engineering. But it is also an art form. "You're painting with light," says Patricia Rizzo, a designer with MSH Visual Planners in Troy, New York. "It's a wow thing."

Such descriptions might seem esoteric to the average person, but when you consider what lighting does, its power to transform a home becomes clear:

Light affects colors and textures as it washes over surfaces. It can make a fine decor look glorious and a so-so interior sparkle. Or it can flatten and muddy the most carefully crafted composition.

Light renders objects into being. In utter darkness, we see nothing. Lit only from the front with a bright, flat light, a sculpture seems two-dimensional. Lit from both sides, it acquires depth and definition. And if we light one side more than the other, it throws dramatic shadows.

Left: For highlighting artwork, halogen bulbs are usually best; incandescents can muddy cool colors. A full arrangement like this is difficult to light without using multiple fixtures.

Right: Two light sources are better than one above a long table. (The same principle applies in a hallway.) Install high-quality dimmers to adjust light levels.

Accent lighting gives artwork starring roles while subtly boosting ambient light. To appear highlighted, an object must be lit at least three times as brightly as Its surroundings.

Light defines a space. When an overhead light fixture illuminates the center of a room, leaving walls in shadow, the room seems smaller. Conversely, when the perimeter of a room is washed with soft light, it feels larger than before. And when a pool of light is partnered with furniture, it defines an intimate area of activity within a larger space.

Light guides our movement. Like moths to flames, flowers to the sun, humans are naturally drawn to light. Soft pools of illumination are both intriguing and comforting. By capitalizing on light's seductive powers, we can transform a home's shadowy realms into alluring destinations.

Light shapes our mood. Lighting establishes the ambience of a space. It not only affects the way we see a room; it also determines the way that we feel when we're in it.

Simply changing all the bulbs in a room can improve the quality of light, but a well-planned lighting scheme involves finesse. The direction, intensity, and color of light, its spread and source all play a role in how a space is rendered. Other factors to consider include the interplay of natural lighting during the day, the way a space is used and, most important, the aesthetic sense of the people who use it. Replacing and refocusing all the fixtures in a home means a new lighting scheme isn't cheap, but it's still one of the most cost-effective ways to change the character and comfort of a home.

{ LIKE MOTHS TO A FLAME,
FLOWERS TO THE SUN,
HUMANS ARE NATURALLY
DRAWN TO LIGHT. }

Mini spotlights in a valence distinguish and define this foyer,
celebrating the homeowner's passion for pottery and plants.

{THE LANGUAGE OF LIGHTING}

Lighting designers have a lingo all their own. What the average person calls a bulb, they call a lamp. What everyone else calls a lamp or lighting fixture, they call a luminaire. Here are some other terms that you're likely to encounter when discussing lighting with an expert:

Lumen: The amount of light a bulb produces.

Watt: The amount of power a bulb consumes.

Line voltage: Regular household current (110/120 volts in North America).

Low-voltage lighting: A system that steps down traditional household current to a much lower voltage (12-volt systems are common). A transformer converts the power. Low voltage generally translates to greater efficiency.

Beam spread: The diameter of the area illuminated by a beam of light.

Wall-washing: Wall-washing is a form of downlighting that bathes a wall in soft, diffuse light using a row of track lights or recessed lights with suitably broad beams. Typically, the distance between fixtures and the wall is 2 to 3 feet, but to fine-tune the effect, both the fixture and ceiling height must be considered. Some people favor a "scalloped" look for drama, while others find it contrived, preferring a flat, even glow of light. And if the light hits the wall too low, the room can look cavelike, spoiling the intended effect.

Wall-grazing: Grazing highlights the textural beauty of a stone or brick wall (or even one with a decorative plaster treatment). A row of downlights are placed close to the wall (typically within 6 to 12 inches) to rake the surface with light. This is not a good technique for ordinary walls; it highlights every crack, pit, or nail hole.

On its own, a central fixture makes a room feel smaller, but perimeter lighting visually enlarges it. Here a lighting valence merges with a red cedar trim line that edges living areas and forms a divider. Uplights provide ambient light; downlights accent artwork.

Key-and-fill: A technique for accenting a sculpture or any 3-D object, such as a column. The light comes from both sides, typically at a 45-degree angle. One light source, the key, is more direct and intense, accentuating form and texture. The opposite source, the fill, is softer and broader, creating a backdrop that offsets unnatural or harsh effects.

Cove lighting: A form of architectural lighting, this term describes a built-in fixture in which lighting and architectural details merge. A soffit, recess, or cornice is fitted with indirect lighting, casting a gentle glow toward the ceiling. A lighting valence is a similar feature; it shines up, down, or in both directions.

Above: Nestled between massive beams called vigas, adjustable copper downlights provide both accent and ambient lighting in this Spanish-style room.

Left: Cove lighting tucks behind crown molding above a wet bar, adding a subtle, romantic glow. A similar treatment edges the skylight over the dining table, eliminating the "black hole" effect at night.

Best suited to light reading and banishing shadows, this accent lamp is rapped in translucent plastic. The lamp emits a warm, inviting glow—and it's unique shape makes it a sculptural piece as well.

LIGHTING TYPES Lighting experts break light into four broad categories: task, accent, ambient, and decorative. Each is defined by its purpose.

Task lighting is the illumination you need to comfortably perform a given task—anything from reading the newspaper to chopping vegetables to playing a game. The positioning of the source and the spread of the light are critical, since the illumination must be free of glare and unpleasant shadow.

One of the first task lights that comes to mind is a swing-arm reading lamp. But a task light might also be a pendant over a small table, or a recessed downlight (or "can") above a sink. Sometimes task lighting requires a pair of fixtures, such as the sconces flanking a bathroom vanity. Or it may come from a series of fixtures: a lineup of pendants above a kitchen peninsula, or microfluorescent tubes tucked under a row of upper kitchen cabinets.

Accent lighting draws attention to a specific feature in a room. Done well, it not only highlights the feature, it also enhances it. The feature may be a plant, a painting or sculpture,

or some other treasured object. But it also can be an architectural feature, such as a beautiful column or ceiling, or a richly textured stone or brick wall. Decor can be highlighted as well, enriching the texture and color of a slubbed silk drape, for instance, or even dramatizing crisp linens on a bed.

By shaping objects and offering relief from an otherwise bland palette of light, accent lights add dimension and character to a space. Choices in fixtures go well beyond the little lamp that clips onto a painting. Track lights, adjustable recessed lights, wall-mounted fixtures, built-in and portable uplights—all are potential sources for accent lighting.

One of the most magical techniques for accent lighting is framing, a means of highlighting a mask, sculpture, or picture on a wall. A framing projector combines low-voltage halogen bulbs with special lenses that shape the beam of light.

Ambient lighting is scattered, indirect light that recalls the soft haze of an overcast day. Though it's sometimes called general lighting, the term "ambient" is more descriptive. Ideally this should be light that's all around, or all-encompassing, without an obvious source.

That light may come from a central fixture that bounces light off the ceiling. But on its own a traditional ceiling light is rarely the best way to create ambient light. The finest effects come from sources that are teasingly concealed, such as cove lights tucked above a cornice. Ambient light also may come from wall-washers, sconces, uplights, and downlights. During the day, windows contribute to a room's ambient light.

Above: The ideal light for shaving and applying makeup comes from the sides as well as above. Sconces should be fitted with incandescent bulbs of roughly 75 watts each.

Below: Cove lights and a quirky pendant enhance the mood of this contemporary home, but recessed halogen fixtures are the real workhorses for general lighting.

A small uplight atop a tall cabinet dramatizes sculptures as it brightens a corner. Normally used to light plants, such portable fixtures are especially handy for experimenting with different lighting angles and effects.

Ambient light can be described as the minimum amount you need to safely move around in a space. But it's also the blending light—a subtle wash of illumination that eliminates unpleasant and eye-wearying contrast between task or accent lighting and surrounding areas.

Decorative lighting draws attention to itself: the fixture is the focus, inviting our direct gaze. While it may contribute to the ambient light in a room, decorative lighting is never bright, because then it would be uncomfortable to admire.

Most designers consider crystal chandeliers to be decorative lighting, preferring to dim them for mood, and cross-light them with low-voltage halogen downlights to bring out their brilliance. Rather than providing any substantial light, a crystal chandelier becomes a dazzling focal point. On the simple side, a string of Christmas lights wound through a grapevine is a decorative light.

The uplight responsible for this dramatic effect is barely visible behind the stand. Its golden wash warms the corner and creates an intriguing shadow play on the wall.

For a fun, magical effect, wind tiny white lights through a free-form wreath made of twigs and bittersweet vines, then suspend it above a dining table. Buy battery-operated Christmas lights to eliminate the cord.

{LAYERS OF LIGHT}

Some how-to books suggest that developing a lighting scheme is a simple three-step process: You start by establishing ambient lighting, then follow up with task and accent lighting. Others suggest that ambient lighting should be the last stage in developing a scheme: It places task and accent lights in context, softening the contrasts between the brighter pools of illumination.

Wired candle lanterns from the Middle East add style to this foyer. Additional illumination comes from wall sconces and table lights. A mirror magnifies the effects.

In reality the categories of lighting are so closely interwoven that they seldom break into such neatly defined stages. "Ambient light is inherent to a plan," explains lighting designer Patricia Rizzo. No single fixture stands on its own. Each contributes to a layered scheme in which softly glowing pools of light help shape the room and define areas of activity within it. Because fixtures can be controlled, they may serve dual purposes: A pendant can be a task light when bright, for instance, or become decorative mood lighting when dimmed. In a small space the task and accent lighting may eliminate the need for an additional layer of general lighting. Determining the brightness and placement of ambient light is a balancing act, one that takes task, accent, and decorative lighting into account.

"There is no one-size-fits-all approach," Rizzo adds. "Every space is different. The important thing is to consider the effect you want to achieve—starting with what you need to see and what you want to see." Then you can design a lighting scheme that fulfills those desires.

Double pendants spread light more evenly than a single ceiling fixture, offering effective task lighting along with vintage style. Recessed "can" lights ensure an even wash of ambient light, while cabinet lights accent glassware.

141

{BEAUTY AND THE BULB}

Pay a visit to a full-service lighting store, and you'll soon discover that lightbulbs come in a dazzling array of shapes, sizes, and types. The light they produce is equally varied, offering choices in color, intensity, energy use, direction, and beam spread. It pays to know the difference. By learning what sets bulbs apart—and taking advantage of those qualities—you'll be well on the way to improving the character of your home.

Incandescent bulbs create a warm, soothing illumination that flatters skin tones and suggests the mellowness of candlelight, especially when dimmed. Although they're the most popular type of bulb, incandescents are woefully inefficient, producing very little light (lumens) for the wattage they devour. Up to 90 percent of the energy consumed is lost as heat. They also burn out more quickly than other bulbs. On average, the annual savings for switching from incandescent to fluorescent bulbs ranges from roughly $10 to $25 per fixture.

Halogen bulbs are a special form of incandescents that create a whiter, brighter light. Halogen bulbs have a number of aesthetic advantages. They make crystal and silverware sparkle like diamonds. And the light renders colors much more accurately than warm light, making halogen the bulb of choice for displays and artwork, as well as any decor whose cool blues and lush greens might otherwise be muddied.

Fluorescent bulbs, for a long time, were maligned for aesthetic reasons. The light they produced was cold and made everyone's skin look sickly. Dimming an old-fashioned fluorescent fixture was not an option; it was either on or off. Furthermore, the ballast—a necessary part of the fixture that regulates electrical current—often buzzed and hummed and the lights often flickered annoyingly.

All that has changed. Fluorescents may not yet match the allure of other

Dimmed for romance, incandescent bulbs produce a skin-flattering light. A backlit panel of frosted glass hides cluttered shelving.

Halogen downlighting adds sparkle as it penetrates glass shelves and reflects off the mirror. Uplights atop the cabinets add glow to the golden ceiling.

bulbs, but they've improved dramatically, and designers continue to make new strides. Electronic ballasts have virtually eliminated the hum-and-flicker problems caused by their old magnetic counterparts. Coatings of rare-earth phosphors (triphosphors) create a glow that mimics the appearance of daylight. Today some fluorescent bulbs even can be controlled by a standard dimmer.

Compact fluorescents are yet another innovation. Here the tube is extremely narrow and bent into a standard-shape bulb, which screws into ordinary light sockets. Straight tubes have slimmed down too. As narrow as a half inch in diameter, skinny microfluorescent bulbs are a popular choice for undercabinet task lighting. Such fixtures even can be linked to create cove lighting.

New technologies are also bringing new lighting options to the home. Among the most promising are light-emitting diodes (LEDs), now available in white. These bulbs are still expensive compared with other options, but they are highly efficient, compact, and beautiful. Small xenon bulbs—cool and efficient incandescents filled with xenon gas—are taking the place of halogen bulbs in many tight spots. Every year dozens of new options hit the market. Lighting designers make it their business to stay abreast of the changes so they can achieve beautiful effects more efficiently and less expensively than before.

{ LIGHT & COLOR }

When bright sunlight strikes a prism, the light breaks into the pattern of a rainbow, revealing a spectrum that ranges from warm red and yellow to the cooler tones of green, blue, and violet.

A white light reveals the spectrum fairly evenly—a quality that allows it to render colors without imparting any noticeable tint. But most light sources don't produce a truly white light. Even the sun has many color moods, shifting toward one end of the visible spectrum or the other. To measure the apparent temperature of light—or its relatively whiteness—scientists use a Kelvin scale (see right). A candle's warm amber glow falls near the bottom of the scale, with a temperature of roughly 2,000 degrees Kelvin (K). On the other end is the cool blue light of a northern sky. Truly white light falls in between.

Northern sunlight gives a chandelier cool sparkle by day, but come evening, the flame-shape bulbs produce a warmer glow.

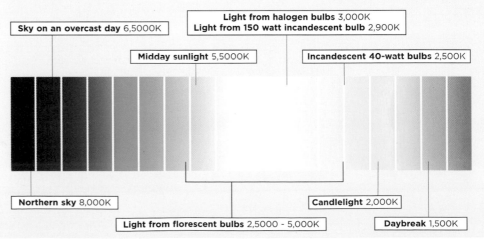

Sky on an overcast day 6,5000K

Light from halogen bulbs 3,000K
Light from 150 watt incandescent bulb 2,900K

Midday sunlight 5,5000K

Incandescent 40-watt bulbs 2,500K

Northern sky 8,000K

Candlelight 2,000K

Light from florescent bulbs 2,5000 - 5,000K

Daybreak 1,500K

Electrical light is measured by the same scale. Incandescent light has a color temperature that falls roughly between 2,700K and 3,000K. (It enhances skin tones and a warm decor, but it sometimes makes cooler colors appear muddy.) If you'd like a fluorescent bulb with similar warmth, look for a similar measurement.

Even within a given category of bulbs, the warmth varies. Low-voltage halogen lights cast a warmer light than their full-voltage counterparts. And a 40-watt standard incandescent bulb produces a warmer light than a 100-watt bulb. Incandescents and halogen lights also become warmer when dimmed (fluorescents, in contrast, hold their color).

A traditional painting light tends to emphasize the top of an artwork. In this case, it enhances the image by emphasizing a soft sky.

{ACCENTING ARTWORK}

When a recessed ceiling light is aimed at a painting, the ideal angle is 30 degrees to prevent annoying glare. The viewer wants to see the art, not the light that bounces off its surface. Other factors to consider:

Ceiling height: The higher the light fixture, the farther it must be from the wall to achieve the correct angle.

Aim point: The focal point of the light beam is typically one-third from the top of the painting—at the average viewer's eye level. To hit that mark from a ceiling fixture, measure the height (H) from the aim point to the ceiling and multiply by .5774; that's the distance (D) from the corner the ceiling fixture should be installed.

Beam spread: The height and width of the light beam should complement the dimensions of the artwork.

Contrast: To appear highlighted, artwork—or any object—must be lit at least three times as brightly as its surroundings. A 5-to-1 contrast ratio, or greater, adds drama to sculptural forms.

Color: Low-voltage halogen lighting is an excellent choice for accenting artwork. It's not harsh, and the white light renders colors accurately.

A lighting professional can help you fine-tune your choices, ensuring you get the right fixture in the right location.

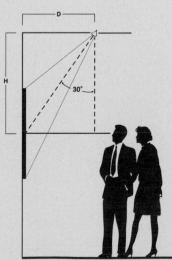

{THE BIG BOUNCE}

When you remodel or redecorate a room, be prepared to adjust the lighting. Dark surfaces absorb light like a sponge, but pale surfaces reflect it, sometimes over and over, in an effect that might fittingly be called "the big bounce."

Imagine that you're in a room where every surface is smooth and pale, like alabaster skin. If you angled a beam of light toward a smooth white ceiling, 75 to 85 percent of the light would bounce back and hit a wall. Because the wall is pale, it too would reflect, angling the residual light toward the floor, which would "bounce the beam" again, until the entire room felt suffused with light. In contrast, a dark red surface might reflect about 25 percent of light at best, devouring the rest.

The upshot: It takes considerably more light to brighten a dark-colored room than a pale one. In a room that is naturally tied to twilight—a formal dining room, for instance—that can be an asset. In a room we expect to be sunny, such as a kitchen, it poses special challenges.

You can tap this knowledge when directing light. If you decide to tuck lighting behind a cornice, for instance, paint the inside of the cornice white to maximize the glow. If you paint a ceiling blue or dress it with dark wood, be aware that uplighting will not be very effective in providing ambient light.

Of course, color is not the only reflector in a room's decor: Polished, glossy surfaces act like mirrors. Conversely, the more texture a surface has—or the more matte it appears—the more light it absorbs.

While pale surfaces reflect light and magnify its effects, these rich red walls absorb it. In a room reserved for romantic dinners, that can be an asset.

{FACTS AND FIXTURES}

Like the bulbs they contain, fixtures come in myriad styles, shapes, sizes, and forms, and most lighting schemes incorporate a blend. Here's a roundup of the basic choices, plus tips for using them most effectively.

A portable table lamp stretches up to admire its own reflection.

More decorative than illuminating, a Venetian glass chandelier makes a design statement day or night.

Portable fixtures. Anything you can pick up, move, and plug into an ordinary wall or floor outlet is a portable fixture. Some, such as piano lights, are obvious choices for task lighting. But others, such as torcheres, can provide ambient lighting as well.

When you're choosing a reading lamp, pay attention to its height: The lower edge of the shade should be at or just below eye level, so the light doesn't shine in your eyes.

Ceiling-mounted fixtures. An easy route to ambient lighting, fixtures that hang just below the ceiling appear in nearly every home, and they can make a strong style statement. A central ceiling-mount fixture seldom provides a pleasing, general light all on its own. If it casts light downward and creates a circle of light in the room's center, it can make a room feel small. Ceiling-mounted fixtures usually perform best when they cast a soft upward glow and are partnered with other light sources.

Wall sconces. Shades are an important element of sconces, determining whether they cast light up, down, or in both directions. In general these fixtures should be about 5 feet from the floor. Space them about 8 to 10 feet apart when lining a hallway or passage.

Track lighting rides the ridge of a long vaulted ceiling, keeping the slopes clear. Adjustable fixtures make it easy to aim lights to wash walls and accent artwork.

Faceted trim gives an old-fashioned flavor to recessed ceiling lights. Install glass shelving and keep interiors pale to magnify the effects of in-cabinet lighting.

Chandeliers. A dazzling accent for dining rooms, chandeliers can grace almost any space. You'll even find them in high-ceilinged bathrooms. Because they hang well into a room and cast light all around, glare can be a problem. In a foyer or hall, they can join forces with other fixtures to provide balanced light.

Wondering how to size or position a chandelier? In a dining area the ideal height is usually 30 inches above the table. The fixture should be scaled to match the table—not the room—without overwhelming it: Experts suggest its outer rim should end at least 6 inches inward from the table's edge on any side.

Above a round table a chandelier roughly half the table's diameter is comfortable. In a foyer chandeliers should hang no lower than 6 feet 8 inches from the floor. If the foyer is rectangular or oblong, a pair of smaller fixtures spaced to accent the room's shape can be more pleasing than a single light.

Undercabinet lights are task lights for the kitchen, but they also can set a mood after the work is done, when other light sources are dimmed. Place undercabinet lights near the front of the cabinet, not the back. The light will spread over your work area better and help avoid glare.

Right: Bendable track lighting can add sensuous curves overhead. A system such as this can take virtually any shape and be fitted with an array of fixtures, from spotlights to tiny art-glass pendants to whimsical lighted airplanes.

Below right: Contemporary halogen track lights brighten this 1920s kitchen, proving that opposites really do attract.

Recessed lights, including "can" lights and top hats, are ceiling fixtures that appear flush with a ceiling. Options for trim (the visible part) vary widely, and they can direct or diffuse the beam of light. Properly positioned, recessed lights can be used for wall-washing and wall-grazing, and accent lighting, as well as general lighting.

Recessed fixtures are prized more for their illumination than their looks. To keep them discreet, don't use widely varied trim packages throughout a space. Today's "can" lights are small and can be fitted with mini reflectors. If you already have older recessed cans, consider retrofitting them with new trim and low-voltage lighting.

Track lights are the ultimate in flexibility, allowing you to re-aim fixtures to suit a changing decor. The individual light sources are varied, ranging from tiny sparkling spotlights to art-glass pendants—all of which can hang from the same track. The tracks themselves can be just about any shape. Cable systems are low-voltage variants of track lighting in which fixtures hang from a parallel pair of "hot" wires. Because the voltage is extremely low, they're virtually shock-free, but it's still best to keep them out of children's reach.

{ TIPS FROM A PRO }

Patricia Rizzo is a designer from Troy, New York, who holds a masters in lighting science from the Lighting Research Center at Rensselaer Polytechnic Institute (www.lrc.rpi.edu). Here are some of her top tips for lighting design:

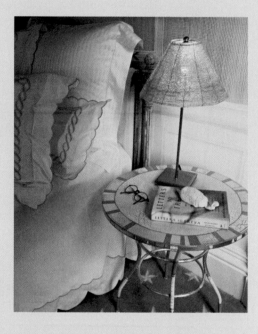

Conceal the light's source whenever possible. Stylish table lamps and decorative fixtures make an important contribution to a room's decor, but discreet light sources have greater mystery and allure. "They take lighting to a higher level," Rizzo says. "It's a much finer approach."

Avoid glare, period. Light should be soft, and it should never shine directly in your eyes. "The biggest mistake in accent lighting is to forget to take the ceiling height into effect." If the fixture is too close to the wall, an angled downlight shining at a painting can reflect into the viewer's face.

Seize control. Dimmers are not just for chandeliers. For maximum flexibility in a lighting scheme, use dimmers on as many fixtures as possible and consider a system with preprogrammed schemes for each room. (A lighting professional can steer you toward high-quality materials and bulbs with strong filaments to avoid the high-pitched whine once associated with dimmers.)

Be kind to aging eyes. As we get older, we need more light to see. [A 60-year-old needs up to 10 times as much light to perform a sight-related task as accurately and quickly as a 20-year-old.] At the same time, older eyes are more sensitive to glare and adjust more slowly to changes in light levels, so a soft, well-balanced scheme is vital.

Position recessed lights to dramatize a bedroom. A central ceiling fixture is "usually pretty awful," Rizzo says. "It's like a big nightlight; it doesn't enhance anything." Instead, set a mood or call attention to objects of beauty. Position low-voltage MR-16s to accent a gleaming wood headboard or heavenly fine linens. Add a few more to make jewelry and perfume bottles atop a dresser sparkle as you enter the room. You'll still want task lights for reading beside the bed, but these can be controlled at the source.

Light bookshelves with ultraslim fluorescents or LEDs tucked into the structure. (They're more discreet than pucks.) For a special effect, make each successively lower shelf slightly deeper than the one above, so the shelves "step outward" at the bottom. Light from a single fixture at the top will cascade down the edges of the shelves.

Accent a beautiful stairway with lighting. For safety, you'll want the top and bottom of the stairway lit softly, but you can also accent the path between. "One of my favorite treatments for a staircase is adding lighted cutouts to the wall," Rizzo says. Instead of the usual photo gallery, carve out geometric niches—display-size squares, for instance—then line the bottom with a translucent shelf and light them from below. They can highlight treasured objects, or be beautiful in their own right, especially as glowing shapes of different color. Yet another idea: To dramatize shapely balustrades, hide miniature strip lighting in a groove beneath the handrailing.

CASE STUDIES

Homes with character don't have to be a given age, nor do they fit the restraints of any single size, shape, or style. Character is as much a feeling as a look—the way a house delights the eye and refreshes a weary spirit, restoring a little bit of what the world takes away.

In this chapter, we'll explore three different houses that have undergone a character-building exercise. Each project is unique, but all share that "certain something": a sense of comfort and grace that lifts an ordinary house above the monotonous fray, transforming it into a character-rich home.

CASE STUDY 1 {CASA BONITA}

Older homes are known for their charm, but sometimes it fades. When Sandy Edelstein spotted this little Spanish hacienda in Los Angeles, its charm had all but disappeared.

An original feature, the fireplace niche features arched openings and a raised, tile hearth. Careful removal of golden paint restored a tile frieze by Ernest Batchelder, an early 20th- century artisan.

{ IF A HOUSE ALREADY HAS CHARACTER, IT'S IMPORTANT TO RESPECT IT. YOU HAVE TO SEE THE ESSENCE OF A HOUSE. }

Curvy metal sconces with an aged finish became a strong motif in the remodeling, continuing throughout the main living areas. Underfoot gleaming oak planks laid on the diagonal visually stretch the space.

Coved edges and a new structural beam accent the living room's vaulted ceiling. A wall of French doors and sidelights (note their distinctive light pattern on the floor) opens the space to the backyard pool.

"The house was a disaster," says Sandy. "The only thing that didn't need fixing was the pool in the backyard." Built in 1925, the L-shape ranch home had suffered through years of neglect and remuddling. The roof slumped badly. Original windows and doors had been replaced with leaky jalousie louvers topped by metal awnings. Moreover, the previous owner's 34 cats had left their marks, turning the house into the kind of renovation project that would make most buyers turn tail and run.

Instead, Sandy turned to designer Robert Young. With help from contractor Roman Vasquez, Young solved the odor and

157

Character upgrades in the kitchen include beams and planks overhead and herringbone-pattern tile underfoot. A pale, subtly reflective finish keeps the 8-foot-2-inch-high ceiling from feeling too heavy.

structural problems, then devised a plan to enhance the home's Spanish style. "If a house already has character, it's important to respect it," Young says. "You have to see the essence of a house—even if it's hidden or there's very little character left—and build on that consistently."

With the house in such sad shape, the entire skeleton was soon stripped bare. New stucco and a tile roof spruced up the exterior, and every window was replaced with a multipane casement in keeping with its Spanish heritage. "We kept the window openings the same size in front," Young notes. "Larger windows wouldn't have looked right on [the front of] this house." In back, however, three sets of French doors were added, expanding views of the pool and giving key rooms ready access to a refurbished landscape.

Although Young gently massaged the floor plan, the home's footprint remained essentially the same. A cell-like maid's room and half bath were transformed into a family room open to the kitchen. Behind the living room, a tacked-on, dark-paneled den was demolished, making way for a poolside patio and a small master bath, the sole addition. "The den wasn't worth saving," Young says. "It was so badly built that it basically fell off." Moreover, it detracted from the home's charm and severed the living room's backyard views.

With the house gutted, Young could have

Top: Claimed from a back bedroom, the family room continues the kitchen's two-tone cabinetry and richly detailed floor and ceiling treatments. French doors just out of view lead to a small terrace overlooking the backyard pool.

Above: Flanked by contrasting cabinets, the stainless steel range is a strong focal point. Tiled countertops trimmed with a wood are a classic but less expensive alternative to solid stone.

finished the interior in any fashion. He and Sandy agreed that the best approach was restoring the home's best features—arched doorways and a coved ceiling, for example—and adding character where it was lacking. In the foyer a mismatched square doorway led to the kitchen, so Vasquez reshaped it to blend with its arching neighbors. (You can create similar curves yourself with the help of a kit.)

Wood and tile flooring laid on the diagonal became a

defining motif. It begins with gleaming oak planks in the foyer and continues in the kitchen's herringbone tile. Occasionally, the pattern appears overhead: In the kitchen and family room, angled tongue-and-groove pine warms up the ceiling, nestling between 6-inch beams. Mainly decorative, "the beams echo the traditional vigas of adobe haciendas," Young says. The planking repeats in the master bedroom, but the beams were omitted to give a lighter touch. For visual relief the living room's oak floor follows the long, straight line established by a massive center beam, which shored up the once-slumping roof.

Among the things the designer didn't add were elaborate crown moldings, or heavy door and window casings. "That wouldn't have fit the flavor of this house," Young says. Instead, most of the trimwork intentionally was kept simple. To add interest to the living and dining room walls, a decorative painter hand rubbed the surfaces with golden-color glaze, then created a tromp l'oeil chair rail using a lacy stencil. Stippled paint and more hand rubbing gave the pattern a worn, well-aged appearance. A matching ceiling medallion accents the dining room's rustic chandelier.

All told, the remodeling took more than a year. Costs soared beyond $200,000, but in LA's strong real estate market, Sandy quickly recouped his investment. The best payoff is how the home looks and feels. With a great deal of work and a little refinement, a ramshackle hacienda became a house of beauty—una casa bonita.

A series of stone terraces and French doors link the house to a backyard bejeweled by a swimming pool. This cozy overlook adjoins the family room.

New French doors transform the modest master bedroom into a poolside haven. Overhead, thin tongue-in-groove paneling echoes the kitchen and family room ceiling, sans beams for a lighter touch.

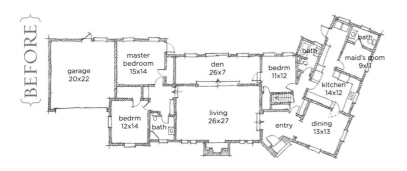

{BEFORE}

garage
20x22

master
bedroom
15x14

den
26x7

bedrm
11x12

bath

bath

maid's room
9x11

kitchen
14x12

bedrm
12x14

bath

living
26x27

entry

dining
13x13

{AFTER}

garage
20x22

master
bedroom
15x14

bath

patio

office
11x12

bath

family
room
14x15

bedrm
12x14

bath

living
26x27

entry

kitchen
14x12

dining
13x13

CASE STUDY 2 {OPENING ACTS}

Like Dorothy's house in *The Wizard of Oz*, many developers' homes seem to land on their empty lots as if they fell out of the sky. Predesigned and sometimes even preassembled, they feel like bundles of little boxes with no relationship to their surroundings.

At the island's corners, the granite countertop steps out to follow the contours of fluted pilasters.

A replacement for a load-bearing wall, classical columns span the opening between this remodeled kitchen and a new dining area. The flat-paneled pedestals end precisely at counter height to create clean horizontal lines.

A single-story addition on the right side of the house includes a mudroom, breezeway, and exercise studio.

That was the story behind Peg and Phil Condon's two-story colonial-style home in Wellesley, Massachusetts. Built in the 1960s, it looked stately from the front, but in the back, a few stingy-size windows overlooked a yard bordered by oak trees and wide-open fields. "It's like a park," Peg says. "Past the trees, the view just keeps going."

Unfortunately the scenery was hard to enjoy. Both the kitchen and breakfast nook were cramped, and neither had access to the outdoors. The family room—actually a den at the far end of the house—felt equally myopic. The plan was choppy and confining, and while the house wasn't shabby, it lacked the rich interior detailing the Condons craved.

The family was ready to make a change. As Peg and Phil's three sons became teenagers, the house became snug, and

when 40-plus relatives visited for holidays, it felt downright tight. So the Condons presented architect John Chapman with a wish list: They wanted a larger kitchen, a roomier haven for casual meals, and a more congenial family room. It wasn't just about adding space, however; the Condons also wanted to add character, comfort, and an easy flow. Chapman's plan gave them that and more.

To enlarge the kitchen the architect claimed space from a laundry room on one side and a breakfast nook opposite. Next he punched through the back wall of the house, adding a dining area that extends 12 feet into the garden. "One of our design restrictions was preserving as much of the yard as possible," Chapman says, "so we kept the dining area small." The space doesn't feel small, however, thanks to a glorious bank of windows and a space-saving banquette snuggled beneath them.

"The window seat is a wonderful place to sit," Peg adds. "And it allowed us to create a broader passageway between the table and the kitchen island."

New construction continues to the right of the dining area, where a family room tucks behind the original den. Shaped like a deep bay with angled sides, the new space boasts a vaulted, multifaceted ceiling. To stretch the apex to 12 feet, the architect positioned the family room floor two steps lower than surrounding rooms—which further distinguished the space. "One of the first things we look at in upgrading a house is the shape of the rooms and the ceiling heights," Chapman says. In the original house, boxy rooms and ceilings just shy of 8 feet were the norm, so the angled family room adds variety on both counts.

Another dynamic turn lies on the opposite side of the dining area, where a dogleg houses a new mudroom, breezeway, and exercise studio. Separated from the main house, the studio

Two steps down, the bay-shape family room boasts a high, faceted ceiling. An angled mudroom (glimpsed beyond) leads to a side entry and breezeway.

Backed by a gang of six-over-six windows, a banquette in the sunny breakfast nook lets the cherry table snuggle up close. French doors, far left, open to a flagstone patio.

WHEN I LOOK OUTSIDE, I HAVE THIS WONDERFUL FEELING OF LIGHT AND SPACE.
—PEG CONDON, HOMEOWNER

lets the Condon boys pump up the music while weightlifting, but its primary purpose was lending privacy to the yard. Although views toward the back of the lot were lovely, a close neighbor on one side made anyone who stepped outside feel on stage. Like a courtyard wall, the dogleg shelters the garden from prying eyes.

Taking full advantage of the seclusion, Chapman nestled a flagstone patio behind the house, accessible through French doors in both the dining area and family room. "I try to show people that by opening up a house [to the outdoors] and investing in landscaping, they can live larger," Chapman says. "An outdoor space is relatively inexpensive, yet it can feel like an entirely new room."

After the project was complete, the Condons upgraded the molding and millwork in the rest of the interior to match the addition's beauty. Tuscan columns became a new motif inside and out. The Condons were so pleased with the look that they later added an elegant portico with columns to the front of their house.

Peg's favorite part of the remodeling is how she feels when she's in the new addition. "When I look outside, I have this wonderful feeling of light and space. The rooms are spacious, but it's also the connection to the backyard. We didn't have that before." Thanks to thoughtful remodeling, the Condons have finally broken free of the box.

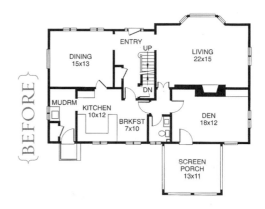

Across the breezeway, a pavilionlike exercise studio helps seclude the backyard. The rough-stone patio is accessible from three rooms, including the exercise studio, breakfast area, and family room.

167

CASE STUDY 3 {SMALL WONDER}

As the saying goes, good things come in small packages. With a little work they can even be wonderful.

A curved cork floor defines the entry, which opened up when an underused closet was demolished. The door's ribbed glass panel introduces a textural theme that repeats throughout the house. A clear section up top lets visitors see and be seen.

{ IT'S SIMPLICITY AND CONSISTENCY OF
BOLD DETAILS AND TEXTURES THAT
GIVE A SMALL HOME RICH CHARACTER. }
—MARK GUNSTAD, ARCHITECT

Layered drywall lends a
simple but elegant detail
to the living room ceiling.

New living room windows expand
views of a wooded glen. The
casements were left undivided to
take full advantage of the scenery.

That's what Jan Mendez and Hal Ekhart proved when they
bought a rundown rambler in St. Paul, Minnesota. Just 960
square feet, the two-bedroom house was nestled on a steep,
overgrown lot in an eclectic neighborhood of character-rich
bungalows and Victorian homes. With its dowdy windows and
big lap siding, the rambler was drab outside, and years as a
rental had taken their toll on the interior. But its location was
right—and so was the price—so Jan and Hal made it their own,
planning to remodel from the start. The only question was how.

At first Jan considered adding a second story, but the price
tag gave her pause. So she and Hal decided to clean things up a
bit, remodel the kitchen, and live in the house for a while. The
longer they stayed, the more they realized that what the house
needed most wasn't extra square footage—it was personality.

Armed with ideas and a wish list, the couple approached
architect Mark Gunstad of Friedell Construction. A graphic
designer, Jan likes contemporary style, and Hal, a metal sculptor,
has similar tastes. But they also wanted their home to blend in
with the neighborhood. Gunstad presented a choice of three
exterior makeovers: one contemporary, one traditional, and
one with Craftsman style. The third plan was the charmer.
With cultured stone wrapping the exposed basement and a
combination of stucco and cedar shakes above, "it just fit," Jan
says. The house already had a matching stone wall in the

Transom windows bathe
the dining room in light
while offering privacy from
a neighbor. A change from
reeded glass below to
etched glass above
underscores the windows'
horizontal lines. French
doors, left, open to the
music room, borrowing
additional light and views.

landscape, she notes. Moreover, the Arts and Crafts aesthetic—which favors clean lines and natural materials—could be readily updated, giving the interior a more contemporary edge without sacrificing architectural continuity.

For Gunstad the biggest challenge was maximizing every inch of the interior to create the feeling of greater space, both real and illusionary. His repertoire of ideas included everything from built-in storage and a bump-out to borrowed views.

At the front door he opened up a cramped vestibule by removing an underused closet, then defined the space with a change in flooring. Underfoot a curved cork inset delineates the new foyer from the living room beyond, which has original maple planks. New windows wrap two walls, reorienting sight lines toward the yard's best views.

More significant changes occurred in and around the dining room. Just 10x12, it was squeezed between the spare bedroom and the kitchen. To visually expand the space, Gunstad

Largely cosmetic, exterior improvements added up to total transformation for this once-nondescript rambler.

Right, top to bottom: Atop a winding stone stair, the new entry porch features flared columns atop stone "piers"—classic Craftsman elements.

The stairway's stunning naturalistic railing was created by metal sculptor Hal Eckhart.

At the side of the house, a deck links the living room and kitchen to a private glen.

Changes to the street facade include deep eaves with heavy brackets, plus new siding of cultured stone, stucco, and cedar shakes. A gabled bump-out over the garage houses the music room's cantilevered window seat.

Sight lines stretch from the music room through the kitchen's westward window. A translucent display niche (on the right) captures light from a side entry.

converted the underutilized bedroom into a music room, breaking through the wall and adding French doors. In the process, the music room acquired an east-facing bump-out with a window seat. Now thanks to the French doors, the bump-out shares its light and views, making the dining room as pleasing for morning coffee as it is for evening cocktails. Sight lines continue into the kitchen, where westward windows balance the light.

In the original plan the dining room's double-hung windows looked south toward a looming neighbor. To solve the privacy problem, Gunstad traded the double-hungs for an entire wall of transoms fitted with ribbed and etched glass. "The horizontal lines help stretch the room," Gunstad says. Now the view stays hidden, and the room basks in a soft, diffuse glow throughout the day. A display niche backed with translucent ribbed glass echoes the design, sharing light between the dining room and a stairwell.

In a move that might seem counterintuitive, the architect dropped the ceiling above the dining room table to 7 feet, suspending a broad panel in the center of the room. Painted

{BEFORE}

master bedrm
bath
bedrm
dining room
living room
Kitchen

master bedrm
bath
music room
dining room
living room
Kitchen

{AFTER}

Above: A marriage of natural maple, reeded glass, and clean-lined geometry, this display niche echoes materials and aesthetics that extend throughout the house.

Left: Custom insets to the kitchen's vinyl floor, blue squares echo the color of the dining room ceiling. The space-efficient coffee bar is a prime bird-watching spot for two.

Below: A back stair links the kitchen to the walk-out basement. Overhead, light spills through a translucent glass panel in the dining room. The sinewy iron rail offers handcrafted character.

{ THE HOUSE IS FILLED WITH SIMPLE, STRONG, ELEGANT DETAIL—FROM THE BIG BRACKETS OUTSIDE TO TILE PATTERNS INSIDE. }

Another space-expanding trick, windows wrap a corner in the master bedroom, continuing above the bed. Bottom-mount shades rise to transom height on the larger windows, offering privacy while preserving treetop views.

a dusky blue-gray, the panel adds intimacy and interest—without any sense of confinement. Hidden uplights reflect off the original white ceiling and create a soft glow around the panel's edges, which stop roughly a foot from the walls. "We call it a cloud," Gunstad says. "You can't see the boundaries above, so it feels as if the ceiling is floating beneath the sky."

In the 10x12 master bedroom, the original closet gave way to floor-to-ceiling built-ins with drawers and tall cupboards with hanging rods, eliminating the need for dressers. There's even a place for off-season clothing, tucked into the highest cubbies. The built-ins wrap a corner and stretch across a doorway, culminating in a storage tower. Serene and uncluttered, the room feels much larger than before, but it's actually smaller. To improve the bathroom's layout, Gunstad stole a few feet from the bedroom's corner.

"The house is filled with simple, strong, elegant details," Gunstad says, "from the big brackets outside to the little details, like tile patterns, inside." Nothing feels applied or superficial. Instead, the details are married to the architectural bones of the house. "It's simplicity and consistency of bold details and textures throughout a house that give a small home rich character."

Above right: A storage tower joins forces with an entire wall of custom cabinetry (right, not shown), eliminating the need for dressers and closets in the small master bedroom. Shelving above the door holds treasured white pitchers, collected by Jan Mendez's mother.

Right: High style on a budget, this custom vanity features two-tone slab doors and a vessel sink atop a black laminate counter. Whimsical striped cones serve as legs, echoing a pattern in the floor tile.

APPENDIX

As with any large project, adding character to your home is a project you can break into smaller, more manageable elements. To get you started, read on for some detailed information about tile, stone, and wood—three elements often used to punch up a home's character. You'll also find seven do-it-yourself projects to give you the opportunity for a hands-on character-building experience.

{ MATERIALS & SURFACES }

To craft a home with character, use classic, natural materials such as wood, stone, and tile. These materials not only endure, they often grow even more beautiful with age. Faux materials aren't always a mistake, but they should be chosen with care. The farther they are from the eye (MDF trim placed high on a ceiling, for instance), the more successful their masquerade becomes.

DESIGNING WITH TILE Terracotta, glass, metal, stone, ceramic, porcelain—tile comes in a dazzling array of materials, with shapes and styles to suit any decor. Before you settle for the ordinary, shop a specialty tile store and surf the Internet to refine your choices. Art tiles are costly, but even a well-chosen few, used sparingly as accents, can add a distinctive touch to your home. (If you're on a tight budget, consider making your own; you can paint or stamp simple organic patterns onto unglazed tiles and have them fired.) In the kitchen stone tile is an economical alternative to solid granite countertops, which require professional installation. Here are some additional tips for working with tile:

Avoid small, awkwardly cut pieces. Whatever surface you're covering, try to choose a tile size that minimizes cutting. When you do have to cut, partial tiles should be at the edge of the surface, where they're least noticeable—not dead center.

Line it up. Grout lines are as important to pattern as the tile itself, and alignment is key. Take a look at the fireplace on page 56. Notice how grout lines continue in straight lines top to bottom throughout the intricate pattern of changing tiles. Think of how disconcerting the look would be if the pattern wasn't followed. Now look at the fireplace on page 65. The variation in tile size causes those up-and-down grout lines to shift but in a neatly repetitive manner. Obtaining this level of consistency takes a lot of planning. The size of the fireplace and tiles has to be coordinated.

Fool the eye. Lay floor tiles on the diagonal to visually widen a narrow room. This trick is often used in small bathrooms.

Mix it up. A traditional stone floor has random sizes and colors, enhancing its textural beauty. Capture that same rich effect by using inexpensive stone-look tile in mixed sizes and subtly different shades.

Know your materials. Natural stone is porous, and must be routinely sealed. Unsealed marble will stain far more readily than granite, so it needs more care (even orange juice can etch it). Ceramic tiles aren't usually suitable for a three-season sunroom; instead, look for a frost-proof porcelain-bodied tile. In a high-impact area consider a tile whose color extends throughout, so chips or scratches are not visible. Around a

fireplace use heat-resistant tiles and mortar; consult with a tile supplier for details.

GOOD WOOD Whether you're talking about moldings, built-ins, or floors, wood is the most popular material. There's a certain sensuality to wood, making it as pleasing to the touch as it is to the eye.

Every wood has a unique personality. Even if you're painting the surface, the differences can be noticeable: Highly textural, the open grain of oak is still obvious beneath a coat of paint, while painted pine or poplar is much smoother. But if you're leaving the wood natural, its color and grain become an important part of your decor. Cherry has a rich, reddish-orange hue that darkens with age (the dark purplish tone of

traditional dark cherry furniture is achieved with a colored stain). Oak is a bit mellower if left unstained, and may be white or red. (Quartersawn oak is a traditional choice for Craftsman interiors.) Maple comes in both soft and hard versions, and has become prized for its pale golden hue. Pine also has a yellowish color, while poplar can take on a yellowish green cast. Fir has a rich, mellow tone that often falls between gold and amber.

While these are the most common choices, exotics and old favorites are also popular choices—both for moldings and flooring. A prime example: Brazilian cherry. Named for its rich red hue, it isn't "cherry" at all (it's actually jatoba wood). The densest of all pines, heart pine comes from the heartwood of old-growth longleaf pines (they now grow in protected forests, so any wood you buy will probably be reclaimed). Golden when newly cut, heart pine gradually darkens to a rich red when exposed to sunlight.

WOOD UNDERFOOT For beauty and warmth underfoot, wood floors are unrivaled, and with new manufacturing methods, they've become increasingly durable and affordable. Even inlays and borders are within reach of the average home-owner, thanks to modern laser technology that cuts costs as well as it cuts wood. If you're looking for a wood floor—or one that just resembles it—here's a quick rundown of your choices:

Laminate floors are look-alikes. What you see is actually a photograph of wood (or stone or tile) glued onto a thin wood-composite core. Topping it off is a clear protective coating. Some laminates look very convincing, but they lack texture and may sound like plastic underfoot. If damaged, they can't be sanded or refinished; instead, you'll have to replace the affected planks.

Solid wood flooring is the old-fashioned, tried-and-true option. It tends to hold its value because it can be sanded and refinished many times. On the down side, it may demand more upkeep, because a finish applied on-site often wears faster than a factory-applied finish. The harder the wood, the better it resists damage like dents and scratches. Of course, some people enjoy the rusticity of a dented pine floor—and since pine is very soft, you might as well embrace the well-aged look if you choose it.

Engineered wood flooring comprises several layers of wood merged through heat and pressure. The result is a strip (or plank) that shrinks and expands less than solid wood, so it can go where solid wood flooring can't, even over concrete in a basement. Topping each strip is a layer of real wood, usually with a highly durable factory finish.

Quality varies greatly among engineered wood products, so if you're considering this option, shop carefully. Compare samples, butting together several planks or strips of each product to see how uniform the cuts and finishes will be across the entire floor. Check warranties for finishes, and assess the wear layer's hardness and depth. (An $1/8$-inch thick wear layer might only be sanded once, but a $3/16$-inch layer might be sanded up to four or five times.)

Prefinished, engineered wood costs more than solid wood, but it's relatively easy to install, and if you consider the labor charges for finishing raw wood, the costs tend to balance out.

{PROJECTS}

You'll be amazed at how quickly you can change the character of a room with a few simple carpentry projects. Here are a few ideas to get you started. For more projects and advice, get *Better Homes and Gardens Step-by-Step Carpentry & Trimwork.*

A WELL-DRESSED CEILING

{MATERIALS}

Pine 1×4s

3-inch-wide tongue-in-groove paneling

1¼-inch panel or screen molding

Putty and paint

If your ceiling is in good shape, or you don't want the casual look of beaded board, simply install the pine 1x4s and paint for instant character.

THE PROJECT:
Create a a ceiling with a coffered look using ordinary 1×4s and trim. For added panache (or to conceal underlying flaws), cover the entire ceiling with tongue-and-groove planking between the "beams." This is time-consuming, back-stressing work with a lot of miter cuts, but it's well within reach of a patient do-it-yourselfer.

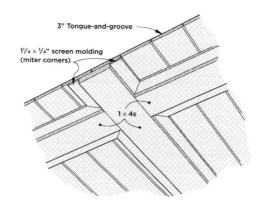

HOW-TO:

- Locate anchoring structures using a stud finder. Paneling and other heavy items attached to a ceiling must be well-anchored to joists, beams, or studs. Mark anchor points for reference.
- Lay out the grid of "coffers," marking it on the ceiling with removable paint tape. (You may want to create a scale drawing of your ceiling and work on paper first to perfect your design.)
- Attach 3-inch tongue-and-groove paneling over the entire ceiling.
- Top with pine 1×4s, using butt joints.
- Finish the interior of each coffer with 1¼ inch panel or screen molding, miter cut at the joints. Tiny gaps and flaws in your joinery can be puttied and painted over.

By simply trimming out the inside of each box of this grid-pattern wainscoting, then finishing the top and bottom with thick molding, you can create the look of expensive paneling.

SIMPLE WAINSCOTING

{MATERIALS}

1×4 pine

³/₄-inch cove molding

³/₄-inch cap molding

Baseboard

Finishing nails

Paint

NOTE: When planning and measuring, remember that nominal lumber sizes are smaller than true sizes. (A 1×4 is actually ³/₄ by 3¹/₂ inches, for instance.)

THE PROJECT:
Create the look of painted, paneled walls with Arts and Crafts flavor using a simple grid atop existing drywall.

HOW-TO:
- To make sure you're getting the look you want, make a scale drawing of each wall. You may find out that what works perfectly on one wall is less than perfect on another. And it's a lot easier to adapt your design on paper than on a real wall.
- On the drawing determine the size of the grid pattern. On this wall the wainscoting covers two thirds of wall height, and the top grid is made up of squares that are about half the height of the rectangles on the bottom.
- Using a level, ruler, and chalk, mark your pattern on the wall.
- Glue the 1x4 pine boards to the wall to create the basic grid pattern. Fasten in place with finishing nails.
- Attach the cove molding inside the frame of 1x4s to give the wainscoting a more tailored look.

- Finish the top of the wainscoting with cap molding and the bottom with a large baseboard.
- Set the nails below the surface, fill the nail holes with wood filler, let dry, and sand smooth.
- Prime and paint.

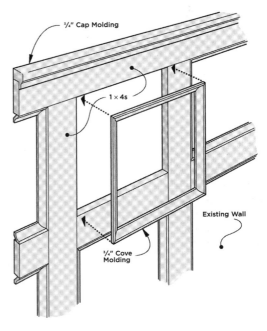

³/₄" Cap Molding

1 × 4s

³/₄" Cove Molding

Existing Wall

Whether you're going for grand, like this room, or simply want to add a little style, the technique is the same. The success is in creating a balanced plan that accents the room's best features.

{MATERIALS}

1×4s for frame

¾-inch cove molding

¾-inch cap molding

TIP: **To make drywall "panels" look more like real wood, brush on satin or semigloss paint that matches surrounding trim. Stippled roller marks won't look authentic.**

PICTURE-FRAME WAINSCOTING

THE PROJECT:

Decorate a room using "picture-frame" wainscoting, or wall frames. Less costly than raised wood panels, wall frames create a classic, elegant look that's appropriate to many historical styles. *Note:* Wall-frame moldings should be significantly narrower than a chair rail or picture rail. Experiment with profiles that complement your decor; flat band molding, wall molding, and contour picture-frame molding may work. The amount required varies with the project. Select the straightest possible pieces to avoid headaches during installation.

DESIGNING A PATTERN:

Options for sizing and shaping each frame vary widely.
- To design a layout you'll need a calculator to determine how many frames fit your space. Planning wall-frame layouts involves trial and error. Here are a few tips for success:
- Create scale elevational drawings of each wall on graph paper, complete with doors and windows and fixed obstructions such as heat registers. Make photocopies so you can sketch designs on top, or use tissue paper overlays.

- Find the wall's center point and work outward. If frames vary in size, it usually looks best if a full-size frame lies dead center, and smaller frames of equal size fall at the ends.
- Ideal shapes depend on personal taste and your room's architecture. For frames stretching below a chair rail, however, horizontal rectangles tend to look best. If frames continue above the chair rail, tall rectangles that stretch toward the ceiling work well. Either way, consider following the *Golden Mean.* A rule of Classical design, it states that the most pleasingly proportioned rectangle is one whose long sides measure just over one and half-times the length of the short sides (the ratio is 1:1.6).
- Frames don't have to be a uniform size across the wall. For instance, when framing extends below a window, you should size the picture frame so its sides align with the window casings. If the window sill is low, the frame's top may be "pushed" lower than its neighbors; otherwise, adjacent frame-tops usually align. Be sure to make your frames large enough to accommodate any artwork or mirrors you intend to hang.
- Spacing around frames is generally uniform. But the space above a frame isn't the same as the space below it. Use a 3:4 ratio—3 units at the top and sides, 4 at the bottom—to determine spacing between a frame's edges and any adjacent molding, including another frame, a chair rail, door casing, or baseboard. (Ever notice how the matts within framed artwork are wider at the bottom? That's the 3:4 ratio at work.)

HOW-TO:

- Mark your pattern on the wall with painter's tape (1). Start with the chair rail (if you're installing one), checking for level. Be sure that each frame is level and square, too.
- Prime and paint moldings before installation. (2)

- Each frame requires four miter joints. Measure and cut moldings using a miter saw *(photo directional)*. Practice cuts on scraps as needed until your joints fit neatly. (Minor gaps and flaws can be filled and painted.) Cut from the thinnest edge of the molding toward the thickest. Sand lightly to eliminate loose splinters.
- Drill nail holes using the same size finish nail that will anchor the moldings to the wall. Apply a thin, wavy bead of carpenter's glue to the back of each molding piece. (3)

- Attach frames to the wall with finish nails. Set nails to recess heads. Fill with painter's spackle, smooth, and let dry. (4)
- Fill any gaps or flaws in joinery with painter's caulk. Touch up with paint.

The warm and cozy look of beaded board is the perfect choice for a cottage-style room. The good news is that it's also quite durable, perfect for preventing dents and dings on walls in high-traffic areas.

BEADED-BOARD WAINSCOTING

THE PROJECT:

Get the look of traditional beaded-board wainscoting using panels or precut sheets instead of tongue-in-groove planks. (Planks have a crisper appearance, but panels are easier and less costly to install.)

HOW-TO:

• Determine the ideal height of the wainscoting. Instead of precut panels, consider buying 8×4-foot panels and cutting them yourself to save money. You'll get three 4-foot-wide by 32-inch-high panels from each standard sheet.
• Read manufacturer instructions for the panels carefully; let *them*—not these general guidelines—be the final arbiter where questions arise.

• Acclimate panels to your environment by letting them sit in your house a few days. (This helps prevent shrinking and expanding after installation.) Stack sheets horizontally with thin spacers between each one for air circulation.
• Draw a horizontal line on the wall at the desired height. (1) Make sure it's level and continue the line around the room. Using a water level is the best way to extend a level line around a room. (2) (Don't just measure up from the floor; your floor may not be level. Your baseboard will cover any gaps between the panel and the floor.)
• After you've marked the desired height around the room using a water level, an easy way to connect all the markings is to snap a chalk line.
• Start cutting panels. As you proceed, carefully measure positions of outlets and switches and mark them on the back of panels. Cut out holes with a jigsaw. (4) (Later, you'll add box extenders to electrical outlets to ensure

wires are contained.) Holes must be sized to fit the underlying box; outlet and switch covers will overlap.

- Paint now; it's easiest to do this before installation, then touch up any flaws later.
- Apply construction adhesive to the back of panels in a zig-zag pattern for good coverage. (5)
- Glue and nail into place. Inset nails. (6)
- Install the cap and base molding using brads and standard joinery techniques for molding. (8) A miter box comes in handy for making accurate angled cuts (7)
- Fill nail holes with putty and caulk gaps as needed. Touch up with paint. (9)

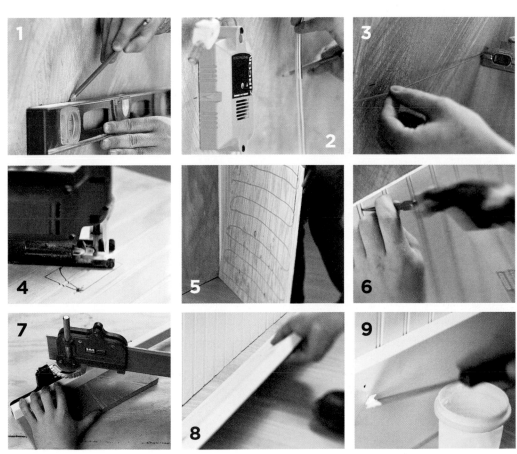

If the profile of standard chair rail molding doesn't appeal to you, create your own by combining standard moldings. Buy short pieces of several molding profiles (cove, half round, etc), and line them up on a sample board until you get a look that you like.

CUSTOM CHAIR RAIL

{MATERIALS}

- 1x4-inch poplar or pine boards
- Cove molding, or inside corner molding
- Half round molding (optional)

THE PROJECT:
Made from stock molding, this chair rail has more depth and curves than the standard chair rail.

HOW-TO:
- Establish the desired height. (Chair rails are usually 30 to 36 inches from the floor.) Mark the rail position, double-checking for level, and snap a chalk line. (1)
- Align a board along the chalk line. Have a helper hold the piece in place, then use a level to ensure the trim is level. Nail the trim to the wall. Repeat around the room. (2) This is the main rail.
- Run a bead of wood glue along the top of the board. (3)
- Set the inside-corner molding or cove molding on top of the board and press firmly into place. Fasten the cap to the main rail with finishing nails. (4)
- For added detail, run cove or inside-corner molding along the underside of the main rail.
- To add detail to the front of the main trim, attach half-round molding just under the top edge of the main rail and just above the bottom edge. Using two sizes of half round will create a more pleasing profile.
- Set all nails below the surface using a nail set. Fill the holes with wood filler, let dry, and sand to finish. (5) Prime and paint.

DISPLAY SHELF

{ MATERIALS }

Pine or poplar board
of the desired depth.

Standard crown
molding

Wood glue

4d finishing nails

Concealable hanging
hardware

Wood filler

Paint

You can make this shelf
as deep or as shallow
as you like simply by
changing the width of
the shelf board. The
wider the board, the
more it extends over the
crown molding base.

THE PROJECT:
Display art pieces and family photos on
a decorative shelf made of trim molding.

HOW-TO:
- Use a miter box and back saw or a
  power mitersaw to cut the top shelf
  board to board to length; standard
  lengths are 2, 3, or 4 feet. (1)
- Cut the crown molding to the desired
  length; the molding should line up with
  the ends of the shelf, but the shelf front
  may extend beyond the molding. (2)
  Then cut the ends with opposing 45-
  degree angles. Measure and cut the end
  pieces to abut the front molding. The
  sides of the end pieces that fit against
  the wall should be 90-degree cuts to
  seat flush against the wall.
- Apply wood glue to the surface areas
  of the shelf and the crown molding.
  (3)Attach the molding ends to the
  molding front, and the shelf to the top
  of the molding assembly.
- Clamp the unit together. Drive finishing
  nails through the crown molding into the
  top of the shelf. Apply glue to the end
  pieces and attach flush to the front
  molding with finishing nails. Set the nails
  using a nail set.

- After the glue has dried, fill the nail
  holes with a wood filler and allow it to
  dry. If the filler shrinks, apply the filler
  a second time. (4)
- Sand the filled nail holes and any rough
  areas starting with a coarse grit,
  gradually working to a fine grit for a
  smooth surface.
- Paint the entire exposed surface with a
  primer, let it dry, and lightly sand with
  a fine-grit sandpaper. Apply the final
  paint color using two coats if needed. (5)
- To hang the shelf use a studfinder to
  locate studs in the wall. Attach a cleat
  to the wall in the studs and fit the shelf
  over the cleat. Secure with countersunk
  screws down through the shelf into
  the cleat. (For more options, check out
  the shelf-hanging hardware at the
  hardware store.)

{INDEX}